Richard Verdi
is Professor of Fine Art and Director
of the Barber Institute of Fine Arts at the University
of Birmingham, England. He organized the exhibition
Cézanne and Poussin: The Classical Vision of Landscape held
at the National Gallery of Scotland in 1990, for which he
wrote the catalogue and received a National Art Collections
Fund Award for an Outstanding Contribution to the
Visual Arts. He is also the author of
Klee and Nature (1984).

WORLD OF ART

This famous series
provides the widest available
range of illustrated books on art in all its aspects.
If you would like to receive a complete list
of titles in print please write to:
THAMES AND HUDSON
30 Bloomsbury Street, London WC1B 3QP
In the United States please write to:
THAMES AND HUDSON INC.
500 Fifth Avenue, New York, New York 10110

Printed in Singapore

1 *Self-Portrait, c.* 1880

RICHARD VERDI

Cézanne

182 illustrations, 33 in color

THAMES AND HUDSON

To my students, past and present

ACKNOWLEDGMENTS

My greatest debt in preparing this text has been to the National Gallery of Scotland for inviting me to devise an exhibition which provided such a stimulus to my own thoughts on Cézanne as to make the writing of this book both pleasurable and inevitable. I am grateful, too, to John Rewald, doyen of Cézanne scholars, whose exemplary life of the artist forms the basis of much of the biographical material included here. Finally, among the many unnamed dedicatees of this volume, from whom I have learned so much over the years, five must be mentioned as having actively assisted at its birth: Nicola Boden, Deborah Holmes, Rupert Knight, Judith Nesbitt, and Judith Showan.

The following abbreviations, employed throughout the text, refer to the three standard catalogues of Cézanne's works: V. (Lionello Venturi, Cézanne, son art – son oeuvre, catalogue raisonné, Paris 1936, 2 vols); RWC (John Rewald, Paul Cézanne: The Watercolours, catalogue raisonné, London and New York 1983); Ch. (Adrien Chappuis, The Drawings of Paul Cézanne, A Catalogue Raisonné, Greenwich, Conn. and London 1973, 2 vols).

© 1992 Thames and Hudson Ltd, London

First published in the United States of America in 1992 by Thames and Hudson Inc., 500 Fifth Avenue, New York, New York 10110
Reprinted 1997

Library of Congress Catalog Card Number 92-80596
ISBN 0-500-20258-3

Printed and bound in Singapore

Contents

CHAPTER ONE

'Difficulties . . . of the first word'

Still life was the ideal subject for Cézanne. It was mute, motionless, and long-lasting. Carefully laid out on a tabletop before him, the fruit, flowers, and earthenware vessels that Cézanne favoured for these pictures permitted him to pursue his pictorial researches undisturbed by the vagaries of man or nature. Given the inordinate number of 'sittings' to which the artist subjected even his most inanimate subjects, however, it is inevitable that Cézanne's fruit and flowers often withered and died in the course of these sittings, only to be replaced by their artificial counterparts.

Still life had another advantage for the artist. It was both traditional and free, sanctioned by the Old Masters and yet largely unencumbered with meaning. This made it possible for Cézanne to build upon the achievements of the past while still pursuing his own unique vision. 'To my mind one does not put oneself in place of the past', declared the artist in 1905, 'one only adds a new link.' To discover the nature of Cézanne's 'new link', it is worth looking closely at one of his still-life compositions in relation to what had gone before it.

The *Still Life with Compotier* of *c.* 1880 is a masterpiece of Cézanne's middle years and bears the artist's signature to prove it. Only thirteen works of Cézanne's maturity were accorded this distinction. The remaining more than 550 canvases were left unsigned, presumably because the artist regarded them as still in need of further resolution.   *6*

In the *Still Life with Compotier*, Cézanne creates a design of monumental simplicity out of the humblest of objects. A bowl of fruit resting on a sideboard is set before a foliage-patterned wallpaper. To the right is a wine glass; while below, additional apples are positioned on a white napkin or tablecloth which projects towards the viewer, a device mirrored by the diagonally placed knife at the lower right.

Cézanne's great predecessor, Chardin, employs similar devices in his *Preparations for a Lunch* of 1763. Like Cézanne, Chardin has   *2* carefully selected and arranged familiar household objects to create an impression of remarkable stability. Like Cézanne, too, he depicts these objects with a sobriety and seriousness traditionally reserved for more elevated themes. But, in contrast to Cézanne, the eighteenth-

2 Jean-Baptiste-Siméon Chardin, *Preparations for a Lunch*, 1763

century master implies a narrative context for the objects he paints which is absent from the *Still Life with Compotier*. In the projecting tabletop, the more distant vantage point, the choice of objects, and (above all) the half-opened drawer, Chardin suggests an unseen human presence in this domestic space and setting which is confirmed by the title eventually given to his work. In Cézanne, one is discouraged from considering the potential utility of the objects presented, both by their non-specific nature and by the equal emphasis given to both still life and setting. This unselective response to the scene before him attests to the greater impersonality of Cézanne's vision.

One of the ways Cézanne achieves this is by distancing himself from a concern with the material properties of objects until he no longer makes distinctions between them. This may be seen if one compares his still life with a comparable work by another artist, Courbet. The latter is an acknowledged master at recreating the

3

8

tangible surfaces of objects through the neutral medium of paint. Thus his bowl of apples and pomegranates – all of them carefully distinguished in colour and texture – appeals to our sense of touch or even of taste. Through their fleshiness and their slight surface blemishes, Courbet's fruit acquire a concrete existence calculated to make us believe that they are really there. While Cézanne's objects possess equal weight and mass, they lack the 'portrait-like' qualities of Courbet's fruit and seem simply to belong to a class of things. Like everything else in Cézanne's picture they are reduced to a common substance and surface texture – that of paint itself. As a result, Cézanne's apples exist in a realm of pure vision which awakens no tactile response in the viewer.

Adding to the physical actuality of Courbet's still life is the bold illusionism of his style, which creates space and solid form with complete assurance, as though unaware of the limitations of the two-dimensional surface upon which it is working. In contrast, Cézanne covers his entire canvas with a dense weft of brushstrokes, linking foreground with distance and asserting the primacy of the picture plane. Thus, his apples appear to engender space rather than inhabit it, and his image lacks the deceptive qualities of Courbet's picture.

3 Gustave Courbet, *Apples and Pomegranates*, 1871

4 Edouard Manet, *Fruit and Melon on a Sideboard, c.* 1866

Rather than urging us to reach out and touch, Cézanne's fruit and vessels inhabit a world alien to our own – one dominated by aesthetic rather than material considerations, and one in which it is the harmony of the composition that we savour rather than the potential delights of the fruit.

A greater overall unity of light and colour characterizes Manet's *Fruit and Melon on a Sideboard* of *c.* 1866, in this respect anticipating the less hierarchical approach to this subject of Cézanne. As a forerunner of Impressionism and an important influence upon Cézanne's early years, Manet's more objective vision may still be sensed in the *Still Life with Compotier*. Yet a number of features of Manet's picture distinguish him as a casual observer of the objects before him and contrast with Cézanne's more resolute and reflective approach to this theme. Among these are the arrangement of Manet's still life, in which the objects are distributed with a calculated informality that (as with Chardin) implies an unseen human presence. In contrast,

5 Auguste Renoir, *Fruits from the Midi*, 1881

Cézanne sets his objects squarely and symmetrically within the frame, where they take on a commanding authority.

Another difference is in the class of objects both artists choose to portray. Manet's melon, crystal glass, lush peaches and grapes, and artfully positioned white rose immediately call to mind a mode of social existence – and elegance – very different from Cézanne's classless arrangement of ordinary things. Moreover, Manet's manner of portrayal appears to take everything in at a fleeting glance, imbuing his objects with a significance which appears only skin-deep. Although Cézanne's still life may arouse fewer associations than his, the objects which comprise it are endowed with a dignity and gravity which belie their humble status. This is attained not through their own intrinsic importance but by the magnitude they assume in Cézanne's pictorial world.

Even further removed from Cézanne's world is *Fruits from the Midi* 5 of 1881 by his friend and contemporary, Renoir. In the latter's picture,

6 *Still Life with Compotier*,
c. 1880

the gaudy hues and glossy skins of aubergines, peppers, and tomatoes recall the bounty and beauty of nature, in addition to reminding us of a culinary speciality of Provence, ratatouille. Compared with this celebration of life, Cézanne's solemn still life appeals neither to our touch nor our taste buds; it arouses no desire. Instead, it inhabits a realm of pure being which permits Cézanne's still-life objects simply to exist.

Perhaps it would be more accurate to say 'coexist'; for a second glance at Cézanne's *Still Life with Compotier* immediately reveals the network of subtle interrelationships which bind together all elements in the picture. The inner rim of the compotier echoes the curve of the glass; the base of the compotier elides with the edge of the tablecloth; knife, table, and tablecloth slant diagonally downwards; the wallpaper pattern asserts itself at the upper corners of the picture, providing an internal frame for the composition; and the inner bases of the compotier and wine glass are 'suppressed' to make way for the central group of apples. All of these alignments and adjustments add to the logic and inevitability of the composition and make every element in the picture respond to all the others. How else to account for the pronounced shadow at the bottom centre of the picture than to assume that it asserted its presence upon the artist's consciousness as a means of anchoring and stabilizing the entire design? Even the choice and arrangement of apples appear carefully determined to endow the whole with an unshakeable stability. The brightest and most multicoloured of these occupy the central axis of the picture. The largest appears at the far right, where it counterbalances the weight of the compotier on the opposite side. And a smaller apple, more muted in colour, rests beneath the compotier, discreetly adding balance and symmetry to the arrangement while not detracting from the commanding importance of the compotier itself.

Adding to the unity of Cézanne's composition is the lustrous paintwork, which serves further to uncover hidden links between otherwise dissimilar things. Sparing touches of grey, white, green, and blue unite cloth, compotier, and wallpaper in a subdued colour harmony against which the intense reds, yellows, and greens of the apples quietly glow. In the pulsing colour of the entire surface, Cézanne succeeds in evoking the variety and vitality of sensory perception and in reconciling seemingly opposed tendencies in his own art. Coupled with a design of timeless authority is a reminder of the ceaseless animation of the visual world. Life abounds, in an image which combines the everlasting with the everchanging, as though seeking to encompass the totality of experience.

If Cézanne succeeds in reconciling these extremes in his picture, he also succeeds in remaining truthful to the needs and limitations of art, constantly asserting the pictorial rights of the flat surface upon which he is working through the uniform brushwork and the saturated and repeated hues. Formal correspondences between foreground and background likewise stress the autonomy of the construction and create a taut cohesion between all elements of the composition. As a result, we are presented not with an imitation of nature but with a recreation of it. Deprived of all those incidental details which might lead us to identify them in life, Cézanne's still-life objects appear as pictorial equivalents of the richness and variety of our own world. Few would deny that they exercise a powerful hold over the mind. But it is one which is determined solely by the devices of art.

This is the essence of the 'new link' that Cézanne added to the chain of tradition. Divesting the objects he painted of all practical and pictorial associations, he sought (in his own words) to 'render the image of what we see, forgetting everything that existed before us.' In this, however, rests the greatest paradox – and challenge – of Cézanne's career: that of reconciling the weight of the past with a genuinely innocent vision. Steeped in tradition, and determined to imbue his pictures with an authority comparable to that of the Old Masters, Cézanne sought nonetheless to reveal the essential beauty of · his subjects, *as though seeing them for the first time.*

In pursuing this goal Cézanne redefined both visual experience and painting itself, and paved the way for the revolutionary art of our own century. But it is noteworthy that he achieved this only by humbling himself before his subjects until he could discover their original state – the state in which they had existed before understanding clouded vision. In this respect, as Merleau-Ponty observed, 'Cézanne's difficulties are those of the first word.'

7 *Portrait of the Artist's Father, c.* 1866

CHAPTER TWO

The Young Romantic (1839–1870)

Paul Cézanne was born on 19 January 1839 in Aix-en-Provence, the eldest child of Louis-Auguste Cézanne and Elisabeth Aubert. His father was a dealer and exporter of hats, who by 1848 had amassed sufficient wealth to buy the only bank in the town and whose fortune left Cézanne financially secure for the rest of his life. Louis-Auguste was also to cast a dark shadow over Cézanne's early years. A self-made man – cold, stingy, and authoritarian – he was later described by the artist's sister, Marie, as 'unable to understand anybody except people who worked in order to get rich'. Certainly there is little to indicate that he understood the character and artistic inclinations of his only son, who in later life would confess that he worked instead to find salvation.

Gentle and temperamental in his youth, Cézanne bore more in common with his mother, who, together with his sister Marie, two years his junior, would appear to have been devoted to him. Another sister, Rose, was born in 1854. Yet even from the female members of his family Cézanne apparently derived little informed support for his creative efforts. When his mother became aware of his artistic leanings she is said to have cited the similarity between her son's Christian name and those of Paul (sic) Rembrandt and Paul Rubens as an auspicious early sign. Had she got her list of Pauls right, and substituted Veronese for Rembrandt, she would also have alighted upon two of the Old Masters her own Paul would eventually most admire. No more able to understand the nature of Cézanne's ambitions was his sister Marie, who in 1911 – five years after the artist's death – confessed to Cézanne's son: 'You are much better able to appreciate the artistic side of his nature and his art, which I confess is a riddle to me because of my ignorance.' In this respect, Cézanne's childhood prepared him well for the three decades of incomprehension and neglect he was to endure as a mature artist.

After an early schooling at the Ecole Saint-Joseph, Cézanne entered the Collège Bourbon, Aix, in 1852. There he proved to be a serious student, regularly winning prizes in mathematics, Latin, and Greek, and gifted with a love of the classics that led him, even in later life, to quote freely from them in his letters. On one occasion, too, he received a prize for painting. But there is no doubt that his earliest inclinations were for literature, and especially poetry. These he shared with another student at the college, the young Emile Zola, one year his junior – and destined to become Cézanne's closest friend.

Together with another of their teenage companions, Baptistin Baille, Cézanne and Zola formed a group of three 'inseparables', regularly making excursions into the countryside around Aix, where they would swim, fish, and indulge in animated discussions about poetry or frustrated dreams of romantic love. Before long, Cézanne was commemorating these youthful outings in his earliest sketches; and, much later, Zola described them in his novel *L'Oeuvre* (1886). 'These were escapes from the world, an instinctive sanctuary in the breast of nature, the unconscious love of children for trees, streams, mountains, for the limitless joy of being alone and free.' Unbeknown to any of the 'inseparables' was the even deeper impression these excursions made upon the young Cézanne. Sheltered in his youth by the bonds of firm friendship, which eluded him in later life, Cézanne was already nurturing that deep love of his native countryside which would sustain him to the end.

In February 1858 Zola departed for Paris to complete his education. In the same year, Cézanne received his baccalauréat and, yielding to parental pressure, enrolled in the University of Aix to study law. Already by this time, however, he was also working at the Municipal School of Drawing in the town. There he drew from plaster casts and the live (male) model under the instruction of Joseph Gibert, curator of the local museum – the Musée Granet – named after François-Marius Granet (1775–1849), the notable painter of landscapes and interiors from Aix, who had bequeathed his entire collection to the city. During these years, Cézanne regularly frequented the Aix Museum, making copies after the old and modern masters to be seen there. Though art historians have probably been over-zealous in their attempts to find precedents for Cézanne's art in the routine holdings of the Musée Granet, it does contain a number of works which anticipate certain of his favourite themes: two card-player compositions (Le Nain and Horemans), a *Temptation of St Anthony* by Teniers, an *Old Man meditating upon a Skull* by Granet, and a still life of a plate of fruit attributed to Cuyp, which certainly caught the eye of the young Cézanne, since he copied it (V. 12).

Bored with his studies of law, Cézanne confessed in a letter to Zola of June 1859 that he dreamt of painting and of a studio and of going to

8 *Bathing*, 20 June 1859. Pen
drawing on a letter to Zola

Paris to 'make myself into an artist'. But such ambitions were to come
up against a formidable obstacle, Cézanne *père*, who had other designs
upon his son's future and who was to hold his ground for two more
years. Unwittingly, however, Cézanne's father provided his son with
an ideal opportunity to nurture his budding artistic talents in this
selfsame year.

In 1859 Louis-Auguste purchased the Jas de Bouffan (or 'Habitation
of the Winds'), an eighteenth-century manor house and farm set in 37
acres (15 hectares) of land on the outskirts of Aix. This became the
Cézanne family residence for the next forty years, its imposing façade
and stately avenue of chestnut trees, adjoining an ornamental pool,
forming a frequent subject of Cézanne's later art. At the time of its
purchase, however, it was the interior of the house – the grand salon –
that occupied the artist's attentions. There, between *c.* 1860 and 1862,
Cézanne executed four large panels of the *Seasons* surrounding a

9   portrait of his father, seated in profile and reading a newspaper. The allegorical paintings of the *Seasons* are executed in a dry and highly stylized manner and ironically signed 'Ingres'. One of them is dated 1811, the date of Ingres's *Jupiter and Thetis* in the Aix Museum, that icon of respectable painting which Cézanne also caricatured during these years (Ch. 50). As the leading academic master of the day, Ingres – whom Cézanne later deemed 'a very small painter' – was clearly a force to be reckoned with, and overcome. In this regard, Cézanne's early *Seasons*, with their conscious archaisms, retain something of the quality of an act of creative exorcism, marking the first of a number of received ways of painting the young artist was to register – and ultimately reject. That this rejection was virtually immediate is testified by the paintings which surrounded them in the Jas de Bouffan: a male bather in a landscape in the manner of Courbet (V. 83) and the aforementioned portrait of Cézanne's father, now in the National Gallery, London, executed in a thick and impasted manner which likewise betrays an awareness of those revolutionary forces which had superseded Ingres in the vanguard of French painting.

In April 1861 Cézanne abandoned his law studies and at last secured his father's consent to journey to Paris and study painting. Zola summarized the dilemma facing Cézanne's father during these years as follows: 'M. Cézanne has seen the plans which he had formed frustrated by his son. The future banker has turned out to be a painter who, feeling eagle wings growing on his back, wants to leave the nest.'

The artistic world Cézanne encountered in Paris in 1861 was one torn by theoretical controversies and stylistic confusion. Its spiritual forebears were Ingres and Delacroix, both nearing the end of their careers and long regarded as arch-rivals. Though Cézanne was already familiar with the chaste, classical style of Ingres, Paris afforded him his first sight of the Romantic art of Delacroix, in which colour – rather than line – was used to evoke a world of fantasy and exoticism that was soon to exert a powerful hold upon Cézanne's imagination. At the time of the young artist's first visit to Paris, Delacroix was applying the finishing touches to his two great murals in the church of Saint Sulpice, the *Expulsion of Heliodorus* and *Jacob wrestling with the Angel*. In these, juxtaposed strokes of pure colour, applied with a feverish intensity, serve at once to unify the entire picture surface and engage the viewer emotionally in the scene.

While Ingres and Delacroix drew their subjects primarily from the imagination, Courbet had revolutionized painting in the middle years

9 The salon of the Jas de Bouffan, the *Portrait of the Artist's Father, c.* 1862,
hanging between *The Four Seasons,* 1860–62

of the century by portraying the world around him. This new
doctrine of 'realism', which did little to ennoble even the basest of
themes, at once aroused the ire of the critics and the admiration of
Courbet's contemporaries. So, too, did his broad, painterly technique
of applying thick layers of pigment to the canvas, often with the aid of
a palette knife, to recreate the material substance of his images. This
technique – which was soon to be adopted by both Cézanne and
Pissarro – was derived largely from the study of the seventeenth-
century Spanish masters in the Louvre, where the exhibition of works
by Velázquez, Zurbarán, and Ribera in the Galerie Louis-Philippe
(1838–48) had suddenly awakened French artists to the powerful
mixture of sobriety and truth in the art of the old Spanish masters.

Courbet's defiant art and personality, which once led him to
proclaim 'there can be no schools; there are only painters', also led him

to be rejected from the Universal Exposition of 1855, where both Ingres and Delacroix were prominently represented. Undeterred by this critical affront, the artist erected his own 'Pavilion of Realism' near the official building – a provocative move that the Impressionists themselves would be forced to adopt in the mid-1870s.

Courbet also continued to arouse the hatred of the jury and public of the Salon, showplace of official painting, where, having won a medal in 1849, he was entitled to exhibit unrestrictedly in what was effectively a market-place for artists and battleground for the critics. In the largest of these annual exhibitions, as many as five thousand works might be hung, frame to frame, and floor to ceiling, with several thousand others rejected by the officiating jury. The latter consisted largely of members of the artistic establishment who valued conformity over originality and typically awarded its highest accolades to moralizing allegories or vast historical canvases comme-morating the great events of the past. In the very year in which Cézanne set foot in Paris it bestowed its highest honour upon the now-forgotten painter of battle scenes from the Crimean War, Isidore Pils. Much more memorable was a work accorded honourable mention in the same year, *The Spanish Guitar Player* by Edouard Manet, a picture of a fashionable Spanish subject painted with a vigour and directness that were soon to make Manet the spiritual leader of the Impressionists – and the bane of the Salon jury.

Reunited with Zola, Cézanne seems initially to have immersed himself in the artistic life of the French capital. He visited the Louvre, the Luxembourg and Versailles, and drew every morning at the Atelier Suisse, an informal establishment, also frequented by Manet, Guillaumin, and Pissarro, where artists could sketch from the nude. He also visited the Salon, which he greeted with a mixture of admiration and bemusement, marvelling at the meticulous realism of Meissonier and the morbid fantasies of Gustave Doré. But, before long, discouragement followed; he saw Zola less frequently and began to talk of returning to Aix. In an effort to forestall him, Zola asked him to paint his portrait. Cézanne accepted this ruse, began the portrait twice, but quickly became dissatisfied with it. One day, appearing in the studio for a sitting, Zola found instead the artist's bags packed and the portrait destroyed. All that remains of the various portraits Cézanne apparently painted of Zola at this time is an unfinished sketch in profile. Pensive and wistful in mood, this was itself presumably abandoned by the artist in a fit of temper or discouragement.

10

10 *Portrait of Emile Zola,*
c. 1862–64

Cézanne's unsettled nature at this period is apparent from an early *Self-Portrait*, made from a photograph of *c.* 1861. The latter shows a gentle and retiring young man, with the intensity of his gaze alone betraying his youthful ardour. But in the portrait Cézanne made from this, the face is lengthened, the bone structure emphasized, the brooding mouth and piercing eyes accentuated – and the effect becomes altogether more sinister. Gaunt, fearful, and dejected, Cézanne here appears as a young man at odds with himself and the world. Witness his confession to Zola in July 1860: 'I am going to speak to say nothing, for my conduct contradicts my words.'

Zola's own descriptions of his friend from this time bear witness to the volatile nature of Cézanne's personality and to that combination of stubbornness and insecurity which was to plague him all his life.

11, 12

23

11 *Self-Portrait, c.* 1861   12 Photograph of Cézanne *c.* 1861

'With such a character, faced with changes of behaviour so little foreseeable and so little reasonable, I admit that I remain speechless and pack up my logic', declared Zola in 1861. 'To prove something to Cézanne would be like trying to persuade the towers of Notre-Dame to dance a quadrille . . . He is made of one single piece, obstinate and hard in the hand; nothing can bend him, nothing can wring a concession from him.'

In retrospect it is clear that Cézanne's obstinacy was also the source of his creative strength and originality. But his uncompromising nature was to cost him dearly in human terms. Even Zola appears to have grown disaffected with him during his turbulent first few months in Paris. 'Paul may have the genius of a great painter', he confessed, 'but he'll never have the genius to become one. The slightest obstacle makes him despair.'

Cézanne was back in Aix by the autumn of 1861, when he briefly took up employment in his father's bank and re-enrolled in the Municipal School of Drawing. There he made a number of studies of 13 the male nude which reveal the extent to which he had mastered the conventions of academic life drawing by this time. Before long, however, Cézanne had grown bored with banking and restless for Paris – and painting – yet again. He had also re-established contact

24

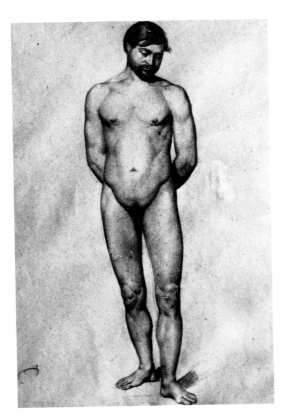

13 *Male Nude*, 1862

with Zola, now at work on his novel, *La Confession de Claude*. 'I approve completely of your idea of coming to Paris to work and then retiring to Provence', wrote Zola to his friend in September 1862. 'I believe that this is the way to escape from the influence of the schools and to develop some originality, if one has any.' For much of the rest of his career, Cézanne was to follow exactly this path, dividing his time between Paris and its environs – where he could keep abreast of the latest developments in painting – and Provence, where he worked in virtual seclusion.

Cézanne returned to Paris in November 1862 and immediately re-enrolled at the Atelier Suisse. There he became reacquainted with Camille Pissarro, nine years his senior and destined to play an important role in Cézanne's creative development. In the following year, Pissarro was one of a number of artists rejected by the jury of the Salon – an event which resulted in a wave of protests from painters

14 Edouard Manet, *Le Déjeuner sur l'Herbe*, 1863

and critics alike. Responding to this outcry the Emperor eventually agreed to a separate exhibition of rejected works – the so-called Salon des Refusés – which elicited only public mockery. Much of this was directed at Manet's *Déjeuner sur l'Herbe*, a large canvas portraying a nude woman accompanied by two clothed men relaxing outdoors. In the background another woman bathes; while to the left appear the remains of a picnic still life. Though the conception of Manet's picture owes much to Raphael and Giorgione, the work was attacked by the critics on both moral and aesthetic grounds. This was for its shameless modernity, which flaunted all the 'rules' of classical history painting from which it appeared to derive, and for its equally revolutionary technique, in which pure, flat colours were applied to the canvas without any intervening shadow or modelling. The result was a dazzling luminosity of colour and tone that assaulted the senses of Manet's critics in much the same way as the apparent indecency of his subject affronted their morals.

Cézanne was deeply impressed by Manet's canvas, both for its bold intensity of colour and its independence of spirit. The picture also earned the admiration of Zola, who visited the Salon with Cézanne and subsequently became one of Manet's greatest champions and a staunch supporter of the new school of painters that grew out of the Salon des Refusés, Cézanne among them. But neither Zola nor any other critic of the time saw fit to mention Cézanne's own submission to this Salon, which remains unidentified to this day.

Resettled in Paris, Cézanne spent the remainder of the decade largely following the pattern outlined in his letter to Zola, spending half a year in the capital and then returning to Aix in the summer, sometimes remaining there throughout the rest of the year. In the summer of 1866 he worked at Bennecourt on the river Seine; otherwise, he divided his time between Paris and Aix and devoted himself doggedly to painting.

Cézanne's early works consist largely of portraits and scenes drawn from his imagination, with landscape and still life – two of the great themes of his maturity – forming a relatively small part of his output. Few of these works are dated or documented and a number of the figure paintings pose interpretative problems as well. Common to nearly all of them, however, is a brooding intensity of feeling coupled with a technique of unparalleled force and immediacy. These testify to the young artist's fierce creative independence and to his deeply disturbed states of mind and have led Lawrence Gowing to describe certain of Cézanne's youthful canvases as 'anticipations of Expressionism'. That these states of mind were largely induced by the artist's struggles to come to terms with his fellow human beings is also apparent from the fact that nearly two-thirds of his paintings up to c. 1870 consist of representations of the human figure. During the last years of his life, when Cézanne shunned humanity altogether, this proportion drops to no more than one-third.

Rebellion – both personal and pictorial – characterizes a *Self-Portrait* of c. 1866, executed with thick strokes of the palette knife, a 15 technique Cézanne repeatedly adopted during these years, as though in defiance of more traditional modes of handling. In place of the mood of lurking menace of his earlier self-portrait, the artist here turns his gaze upon the viewer, sporting what came to be seen as his 'revolutionary beard', in a truculent manner which (as Gowing has observed) reveals 'a ferocity that speaks of refusal to brook the slightest opposition.' Scarcely less uncompromising are a series of likenesses – both bust-length and half-length – of these same years of the artist's uncle, Dominic Aubert, which show him assuming a

16   number of disguises, as jurist, monk, and artisan, as though to fuel the
young artist's love of fantasy. Painted with a palette knife, often in no
more than half a day, these possess an almost unbearable fixity and
appear utterly expressionless in their gaze, suggesting that Cézanne
could not bring himself to relax even before this most obliging family
sitter. But the chief documents of his early portrait style are the three-
quarter length portrait of his friend, the poet and critic Antony
Valabrègue, submitted to the Salon of 1866, and the full-length
portrait of his father reading in an armchair, probably of the same
19, 7   year.

    The portrait of Valabrègue is executed with a crude, almost
cloddish force which seems a conscious affront to the Salon jury, who

28

15 (left) *Self-Portrait,*
c. 1866

16 *Portrait of Uncle*
Dominic, c. 1866

needless to say rejected it – an event which prompted a vituperative letter from the artist demanding the re-establishment of the Salon des Refusés and refusing to accept 'the unorthodox judgment of colleagues to whom I myself have not given the task of appraising me.' Though Cézanne's plea fell upon deaf ears, the indignation aroused by the widespread rejection of the 1866 jury (Manet and Renoir were also refused in this year) prompted Zola, recently appointed literary editor of the Paris daily *L'Evénement*, to take up his pen in defence of the new painters. Denouncing the Salon as 'a mass of mediocrity', Zola put forward his view that 'a work of art is a corner of nature seen through a temperament', doubtless reflecting in this his frequent conversations with Cézanne over the true aim of painting.

17 *Christ in Limbo*, c. 1867

Though Zola's articles served only to incense the public further, they succeeded in consolidating his position as spokesman for the younger generation of painters.

In the same year Zola gathered together all of these articles into a pamphlet which he published as *Mon Salon* and prefaced with a long dedication to his boyhood friend, Cézanne. 'For ten years we have been speaking of art and literature', observed Zola, '. . . searching the past, questioning the present, trying to find the truth and to create for ourselves an infallible and complete religion.'

It was perhaps in gratitude for Zola's championship that Cézanne chose to portray his father reading the newspaper in which Zola had published his revolutionary ideas on art in his most ambitious and accomplished portrait to date. (Cézanne's father did not read *L'Evénement* but rather its conservative rival, *Le Siècle*.) His legs crossed and eyes lowered, Louis-Auguste resists the artist's gaze, an image of domestic contentment and bourgeois respectability – except, that is, for the radical newspaper his son has painted him reading and the equally radical still life by Cézanne himself which hangs on the back wall (*Sugar Pot, Pears, and Blue Cup*, now in the Musée Granet). As a self-conscious expression of Cézanne's own desire for paternal acceptance, this work could scarcely be bettered; for, indirectly at least, it shows Cézanne's father embracing both Cézanne and Zola. Yet that this was nothing more than an exercise in creative wish-fulfilment is apparent from the opening lines of a letter from Cézanne to Pissarro of this same year: 'Here I am with my family, with the most disgusting people in the world, those who compose my family stinking more than any. Let's say no more about it.' Crude as are Cézanne's words, they betray a painful personal

18 *Sorrow*, or *Mary Magdalene*, c. 1867

alienation from his roots – and from humanity at large – that was to afflict him all his life.

This is nowhere more apparent than in the artist's early subject pictures, with their deeply personal imagery and prevailingly sombre mood. In contrast to his youthful portraits, however, these works are unthinkable without an awareness of the art of the past – one which Cézanne cultivated through his studies in the Louvre and his habit of collecting prints and illustrated histories of art, as though constantly aware of the tradition upon which his own achievement was to be built. Though many young artists of his generation and earlier had copied the great masters in the Louvre, in Cézanne's case this became a lifelong pursuit, which even in a book of this size demands a chapter to itself (see chapter six). But if Cézanne drew inspiration from the past throughout his life, his most direct links with tradition occur at the start of his career, when he based a number of his most important works upon earlier paintings.

Cézanne first registered for permission to copy in the Louvre in November 1863. By April of the following year he was making a copy of Poussin's *Arcadian Shepherds*; and, in the same year, he apparently completed a copy after Delacroix, conceivably after the latter's *Barque of Dante* (V. 125), which hung in the Luxembourg. In 1864–65 he also executed a drawing after Rubens's *Apotheosis of Henry IV*, a work which was to fascinate him to the end of his career. From this fragmentary evidence it is clear that the young Cézanne was most attracted to the great masters of the Baroque and to the nineteenth-century painter who owed most to Rubens's colour and dynamism, Delacroix.

136

The fruits of these studies are readily apparent in Cézanne's own figure pictures of the 1860s. One of these – *Christ in Limbo* of *c.* 1867 – is based on a painting by the Venetian Renaissance artist, Sebastiano del Piombo, which Cézanne knew in reproduction (the original hangs in the Prado). Cézanne's copy of this work originally formed the left-hand portion of a large painting that decorated a wall of the salon at the Jas de Bouffan. On the right was a portrayal of the penitent Magdalene, which may in turn have been inspired by Domenico Fetti's painting of the same theme in the Louvre. Together the two formed a traditional Easter subject revealing the rewards (in the form of salvation on the left) awaiting the repentant or faithful (on the right). Though the disparities in scale between the two halves of the composition result in a certain visual incongruity, these have been explained by Cézanne's desire to distinguish between the underworld

17

18

32

19 *Portrait of Antony Valabrègue*, 1866

20 *The Rape*, 1867

and the temporal world. Scarcely less disconcerting is the bold and impassioned handling of these pictures and the abject misery of the figure of the Magdalene, who appears at least as much in the throes of death as in those of prayer and typifies the emotional extremism of so much of Cézanne's early art.

Cézanne's early desire to master the traditional themes of the past is also apparent in *The Rape*, which Mary Tompkins Lewis has identified as a depiction of Pluto abducting Proserpina, who will become his consort in the underworld. In the left middle distance one of Proserpina's companions holds the girdle she dropped when Pluto captured her; while beyond appears the lake and looming profile of Mount Etna so vividly described by Ovid (*Metamorphoses*, V). In the heroic scale and interweaving poses of the figures, and the exaggerated musculature of Pluto, Cézanne reveals an awareness of the rhetoric of classical abduction scenes by such earlier masters as Niccolò dell'Abbate and Rubens, both of whom likewise favoured

20

the clearly differentiated skin tones Cézanne employs to distinguish male from female, victor from vanquished. In Cézanne's case, however, the pallid hues and swooning pose of Proserpina transcend the violent passions of the theme and link sexual desire with death, even in this most traditional of the artist's early subject pictures.

This morbid equation occurs frequently in Cézanne's art of the 1860s, in vicious scenes of sexual violation which culminate in murder or in the menacing presence of a human skull on a sheet of studies of lecherous males advancing upon a recoiling female nude. It also 21 occurs in a dark fantasy Cézanne recounted to Zola in a letter of December 1859, in which a temptress reveals herself to the artist in the midst of a haunted, nocturnal landscape, only to turn into a cadaver at the point of seducing him. Moreover, it is a macabre fascination which Cézanne shared with Zola. In the latter's novel, *Thérèse Raquin*, the heroine and her lover conspire to murder her husband in order to gratify their own desires. Though the lurid events of Zola's novel bear no direct relation to the theme of Cézanne's painting, its morbid passions do. Perhaps it is no mere coincidence that the artist executed *The Rape* in Zola's house and presented it to his friend in the very year in which *Thérèse Raquin* was published, 1867.

Echoes of Zola's novel also appear in Cézanne's *Preparation for a Funeral* of c. 1868, in which two figures prepare a corpse for burial 22

21 Page of studies, 1865–69

22 *Preparation for a Funeral, c.* 1868

against a sombre, nocturnal setting. The scene is arranged like a Lamentation over the dead Christ and takes the form of a monumental predella panel, recalling in its lugubrious hues and stark realism any number of depictions of this theme by Ribera, whom Cézanne is recorded as admiring as early as 1865. Likewise reminiscent of Ribera – and even more of his contemporary Zurbarán – is the rigid angularity of the poses in Cézanne's picture, which lends to it such a throttled intensity. Together with the coiling contours of the forms and the brutal force of the handling, this results in a tragic image of remorseless death which may well have had some deep, private significance for Cézanne. Nor can one ignore the clear resemblance between the bald, bearded figure in the centre of this picture and Cézanne himself at this stage of his career. As M.L. Krumrine has observed, however, these facial features also distinguish the painter Laurent, villain of Zola's *Thérèse Raquin* and himself partly modelled on Cézanne, who after murdering Thérèse's husband visits the morgue in search of his corpse. As in so many other subject pictures of this period, Cézanne here combines traditional and

36

contemporary elements in a style of such uncompromising power and originality that it seems to stand outside of its time.

Two other of Cézanne's most ambitious early subject pictures take their themes from Flaubert's *Temptation of St Anthony*, published in 1874 but first issued in serial instalments in *L'Artiste* in 1857–58. Cézanne's admiration for Flaubert is well documented and hardly surprising; for, like the artist himself, the author of *Madame Bovary* followed a creative path which moved from the unbridled fantasy and romanticism of his youth to the chastening classicism of maturity. Manifestly indebted to the writer's early imagery are Cézanne's own *Temptation of St Anthony* and *The Feast* or *The Orgy*. The former is the artist's first rendering of a theme to which he would return in his middle years – that of the hermit saint vanquishing the temptations of the devil, here personified by three nude women of a brooding, almost repellent sensuality. At the upper left appears St Anthony, doing battle with a fourth female. Painted in sweeping strokes of the brush, in what Cézanne crudely described as his *couillarde* manner, the picture is among the most disturbing and confessional of his early works. More than any other canvas of this time, it reveals the extent to which Cézanne's own repressed desires appear to have been regarded by him as repugnant – even sinful.

In *The Feast* Cézanne portrays the banquet of Nebuchadnezzar from Flaubert's novel, in which the hermit saint is tempted by a vision

23, 24

23 *The Temptation of St Anthony, c.* 1870

of wealth and luxuriant living. With its light tone and coruscating colour, the picture recalls the opulent banqueting scenes of Veronese, not least the *Marriage at Cana* in the Louvre, from which the artist made two drawings during these years (Ch. 168 & 169). But neither Veronese nor Flaubert anticipates the gratuitous brutality of Cézanne's vision, which is treated less like a feast than a scene of open conflict in which luxury leads inexorably to lust and lust to violence in a manner reminiscent of Delacroix's *Death of Sardanapalus*, also copied by Cézanne during this period (Ch. 141). Only the flickering, Venetian-inspired colour of *The Feast* mitigates against this and signals a shift from the darker and more sombre pictures of the immediately preceding phase.

14
25, 26

Two of Cézanne's most enigmatic subject pictures of *c.* 1870 likewise reveal an awareness of the sixteenth-century Venetian tradition, this time as reinterpreted by Manet in *Le Déjeuner sur l'Herbe*. One of these bears the same title as Manet's picture; the other is commonly known as *Pastoral* or *Idyll*. Both portray a group of languorous figures in an outdoor setting in the manner of Manet's composition. In the *Déjeuner sur l'Herbe* the action centres upon a standing female figure holding an apple who gazes in the direction of a seated man clearly recognizable as Cézanne. The unmistakable presence of the artist himself is likewise apparent in the *Pastoral*, where Cézanne reclines on the bank of a lake, head in hand, in a familiar melancholic pose. Surrounding him are three female nudes and two clothed males whose relaxed and abandoned attitudes contrast with the brooding and introspective mood of the artist himself. Though the precise scenario of both of these pictures remains unclear, certain features unite them. The presence of a woman proffering an apple in one and female nudes in the other indicates that both are concerned with sensual longing or temptation and with the artist's deep-seated frustration at expressing these desires, except as they may be sublimated into art. This is apparent in the ominous landscape settings in which Cézanne places these private fantasies and in the tensions which inform the figures within them. Particularly noteworthy is his refusal to permit the figures to interact or even overlap. Instead, they are set side by side in a sequence of isolated poses, as though imprisoned in their own world. So familiar is this device in early Cézanne that it might easily be dismissed as a compositional ineptitude were it not for the fact that the artist overcomes it in works

20, 24

like *The Rape* or *The Orgy*, where the figures overlap and interact to an inevitably brutal and violent end. Otherwise, humanity stands

24 *The Feast*, or *The Orgy*, *c.* 1870

25 *Le Déjeuner sur l'Herbe, c.* 1870

26 *Pastoral,* or *Idyll, c.* 1870

alone and apart in early Cézanne, incapable of contact or communication.

If the dark, erotic undertones of these pictures are already familiar from the artist's earliest subject paintings, one feature of them is new. This is their mood of calm and apparent restraint – one which no longer translates sexual desire into physical violence, temptation into aggression. This transformation may be explained by a change in Cézanne's own circumstances around 1870 – one which led to a period of greater emotional stability in his life, assuaging his own physical desires and eventually providing him with a measure of tranquillity which made it possible for him to abandon the turbulent style and subjects of his earliest pictures in favour of a more objective vision.

Around 1869 Cézanne made the acquaintance of Hortense Fiquet, a model from the Jura, eleven years his junior, with whom he began a liaison which would eventually lead to the birth of a son in 1872. Little is known of Hortense, who came from a humble background and in later life often lived apart from her husband, preferring the animated social life of Paris to the dull provincialism of Provence. From the references to her in Cézanne's surviving letters it would appear that she became a dutiful – rather than devoted – companion, chiefly regarded by the artist as the mother of his much adored son. Evidence of her patience and forbearance with Cézanne may be seen in the numerous occasions when she sat for him in the ensuing two decades. But proof of the fundamental divide between them is the fact that she took little or no interest in her husband's art, even claiming after his death that 'Cézanne didn't know what he was doing'.

If Cézanne's relationship with Hortense afforded him a measure of personal stability, his creative independence remained unaffected by this sudden change of fortune. In 1870 the artist submitted two canvases to the Salon jury. The first of these was a large painting of a reclining female nude, since lost, which was manifestly inspired by another of Manet's most controversial works, the *Olympia* of 1863. Accompanying it was a life-size portrait of his friend and fellow painter, Achille Emperaire, a tragically misshapen dwarf who was to *30* become one of the few boyhood friends with whom the artist remained on intimate terms throughout his life. Not surprisingly, both works were rejected by the Salon jury. As a further indignity, Cézanne was 'interviewed' in the course of his submission and subsequently ridiculed in the Paris weekly, the *Album Stock*, which reproduced a caricature of the artist brandishing his two rejected *29*

canvases and printed below this an account which includes Cézanne's own defiant words at this latest critical rebuff:

> The artists and critics who happened to be at the Palais de l'Industrie on 20 March, the last day for the submission of paintings, will remember the ovation given to two works of a new kind . . . Courbet, Manet, Monet, and all of you who paint with a knife, a brush, a broom or any other instrument, you are outdistanced! I

27 *Head of Achille Emperaire, c.* 1867–70

28 *Head of Achille Emperaire, c.* 1867–70

29 *Album Stock* caricature of Cézanne, 1870

30 *Portrait of Achille Emperaire, c.* 1868–70

31 *Still Life with Green Pot and Pewter Jug, c.* 1869–70

have the honour to introduce you to your master, M. Cézannes[*sic*]
. . . Cézannes hails from Aix-en-Provence. He is a realist painter
and, what is more, a convinced one. Listen to him rather, telling me
with a pronounced *provençal* accent: 'Yes, my dear Sir, I paint as I
see, as I feel – and I have very strong sensations. The others, too, feel
and see as I do, but they don't dare . . . they produce Salon pictures
. . . I dare, Sir, I dare . . . I have the courage of my opinions – and he
laughs best who laughs last!'

If Cézanne's remarks to the jury show him at his most rancorous,
the moving portrayal of Emperaire reveals him at his most humane.
Seated in the same floral-patterned armchair in which Cézanne had
painted his father three or four years earlier, the pathetically deformed
Emperaire, his soulful eyes staring vacantly out into space, appears to
bear the burden of all humanity. It is as though in confronting obvious
weakness Cézanne could express a love and pity otherwise kept firmly

44

32 *Still Life with a Black Clock, c.* 1869–70

in check before more 'ordinary' sitters. Emperaire's compliant nature, together with Cézanne's affection for him, may also account for the ambitious nature of this portrait, with its timeless, 'Byzantine' presentation of the sitter, posed frontally and identified above by stencilled lettering, a device which adds to the hieratic character of the whole. The formality of the image is further enhanced by the strict sequence of parallel lines which inform all elements of the composition – the lines of the chair, pleats of the dressing gown, legs, fingers, even the stencilled letters themselves.

This search for a prevailing structural order is also apparent in a preparatory drawing for the portrait, in which eye and ear, collar *27* and cheek appear aligned in a grand, almost ghostly symmetry. In contrast to this, however, is another drawing of Emperaire in which *28* flowing curves describe the head and reveal its underlying tenderness and frailty. If the first work reveals Cézanne's search for formal order, the second demonstrates his desire for rhythmic continuity in his

33 *Overture to Tannhäuser*, *c.* 1869–70

subjects. Both of these tendencies were to form the basis of his mature art and already contribute to the prevailing unity and simplicity of the portrait of Emperaire.

The rigid principles of compositional order and control of this picture also inform Cézanne's genre portraits in an interior of these same years, the two versions of *Alexis reading to Zola* (V. 117 & 118) and the so-called *Overture to Tannhäuser*. These draw their inspiration from a third great tradition of naturalistic art, which, along with the Venetian and Spanish schools, preoccupied French painters of the mid-nineteenth century: namely, the Dutch seventeenth-century school. This is particularly apparent in the first version of *Alexis reading to Zola*, where the artist frames the composition with a curtain in the manner of a genre scene by Dou or Vermeer and places his figures in a clearly defined architectural setting reminiscent of de Hooch, who likewise favoured the red, brown, and grey colour harmonies Cézanne adopted for this picture. The scene shows the boyhood friend of Zola and Cézanne, Paul Alexis, reading to the former in a gloomy interior lit from a window at the left – another favourite Dutch device. Though such an occurrence is perfectly plausible given the literary ties which drew Alexis to Zola, the self-

34

absorbed nature of the figures in both versions of this subject and in the related *Overture to Tannhäuser* recalls Cézanne's earlier portraits of his father reading and prefigures his later card-player compositions as an image of human isolation and withdrawal.

In the *Overture to Tannhäuser* the artist portrays two female figures, *33* reputed to be his mother and his sister Marie, seated in a room at the Jas de Bouffan, the elder sewing and the younger playing a piano transcription of the overture by Wagner that had taken Paris by storm in 1860. Cézanne himself was an avowed admirer of Wagner's music, around which so many of the most progressive spirits in French painting, poetry, and music rallied during these years. And, despite its unassuming domestic theme, the *Overture to Tannhäuser* remains one of his most revolutionary early works, both for its abstract formal unity and colouristic harmony. Confined to a colour chord of blacks, browns, greys, and whites, in the manner of a Manet or a Whistler,

34 *Alexis reading to Zola, c.* 1867–69

35 *The Railway Cutting*, 1869–70

36 Photograph of the Railway Cutting

the picture is further unified by the most intricate sequence of formal correspondences so far encountered in Cézanne's art. Vertically divided in half by the line of the couch, the scheme is further articulated by a rhythmic sequence of interlocking orthogonals which link background with foreground in an almost wilfully constraining manner. Thus, the pleats of Madame Cézanne's dress align themselves with the lines of the carpet and keyboard; the erect pose of Marie is repeated in the familiar family armchair at the right and mirrored in that of the piano itself; and the coiffure of both women echoes the rhythmic arabesques of the wallpaper and armchair to result in a tautly integrated whole. Though it is tempting to see such a seamless composition as a tribute to the through-composed nature of Wagner's music, it probably results from an increased desire on Cézanne's part (also evident in the portrait of Emperaire) to make all elements of the composition conform to a predetermined order which enforces a logic upon the construction. The effect in the *Overture to Tannhäuser* is to reduce humanity itself to the status of still life in a manner that anticipates Matisse's most radical innovations of forty years later.

Cézanne's still lifes of the 1860s reveal a comparable search to impose abstract principles of formal design upon the most ordinary things. The earliest original work among them is probably the *Still Life with Bread and Eggs* of 1865. In this the young artist reveals his 37 affinities with those mid-nineteenth century artists, such as Ribot and Bonvin, who had revived an interest in the art of Chardin. Employing a largely monochromatic palette, Cézanne assembles a group of domestic objects on a tabletop, as though in preparation for a simple meal, and paints them with a sobriety and realism which stand in marked contrast to the agitated handling of his early figure pictures. The latter style re-emerges, however, in a *Still Life with Skull and Candlestick* of c. 1866, executed with a palette knife. Here Cézanne 38 portrays the traditional objects of a *vanitas* still life, complete with open book and dying flower, in a technique so brutal and 'decaying' as to redouble the morbid symbolism of the theme. Adding to the confrontational nature of the picture is the centrally placed skull, its dark sockets staring out at the viewer with menacing authority.

Though Cézanne painted a handful of less portentous still lifes of the mid-1860s in a similarly charged manner, by the end of the decade he had adopted a more impersonal handling for this most reticent of pictorial themes. In this style he executed two undisputed master works, the *Still Life with Green Pot and Pewter Jug* and the *Still Life with* 31, 32

49

37 *Still Life with Bread and Eggs*, 1865

a Black Clock. The former returns to the familiar household objects of
the 1865 picture, now rendered with a clarity and authority which
lend them an epic seriousness. In the earlier work Cézanne reveals a
lingering concern with textural variations and phenomenal light
effects which still link him with the realist tradition of the mid
century. In the picture of *c*. 1870, however, these concerns are
abandoned and all elements of the composition appear hewn out of
paint with a strength and assurance that calls to mind the early
bodegónes of Velázquez, as do the saturated, earthy hues.

Even more remarkable is the *Still Life with a Black Clock*, perhaps
the most successful reconciliation among Cézanne's early pictures of
those contending currents of classicism and romanticism that were to
wage war within him throughout his career. The picture portrays a
fluted vase, cup, and lemon flanked on one side by a clock that
belonged to Zola and, on the other, by a conch shell, whose bright red

38 *Still Life with Skull and Candlestick*, c. 1866

opening and scalloped contours add an unexpected note of drama and fantasy to the scene, reminiscent of the romantic exoticism of many of the artist's early figure paintings. The design itself, however, could hardly be more defiantly classical. Rising below from the broad panel-like divisions of the tablecloth, indented with horizontal pleats echoing the stripe on the teacup and the mouth of the shell, it culminates in a symmetrical grouping of objects of sovereign authority. As in the *Overture to Tannhäuser*, Cézanne here asserts his will upon the composition until all elements cohere, the convoluted contours of shell, vase, and tablecloth at the right contrasting with the emphatic vertical and horizontal accents which dominate the rest of the picture. The result is a grandeur and finality of conception and execution that arguably surpass anything Cézanne had attained in figure painting by this time. It reminds us that, in the more impersonal art of still life, he was often to make his greatest creative strides.

39 *Landscape with the Tower of Caesar*, 1860–61

Closely paralleling Cézanne's development as a still-life painter in the 1860s is his evolution as a landscapist. Though this theme would eventually outnumber all others in his art, its beginnings are decidedly modest. Only about two dozen landscapes may be assigned to the first decade of Cézanne's career. The majority of these are small in scale and portray scenes of rural nature undisturbed by humanity. Many of them are executed with a palette knife, a technique which owes much to the art of Courbet and Pissarro and has close affinities with Cézanne's figure paintings of this period. In one of the earliest of

39   them, however, the *Landscape with the Tower of Caesar* of 1860–61, the artist depicts a hillside site outside Aix in the manner of Corot or Granet. Like the atmospheric landscape *études* of both of these masters, Cézanne's picture is executed on paper laid down on canvas – a technique widely adopted by naturalistic landscape painters of the early nineteenth century for capturing fleeting impressions directly from nature. Painted with broad, fluid strokes, in a subtle range of greys and greens, the work reveals a restraint and receptivity to nature also characteristic of Corot and his followers. But the choice of vantage point already foretells the future Cézanne. Centred around a solitary cottage and cypress, the scene is bounded on either side by the

52

40 *View of Bonnières*, 1866

converging diagonals of the flanking hills to give it a balance and symmetry which preclude any suggestion of a chance encounter or a purely picturesque intention.

Cézanne adopts the same basic scheme for his *View of Bonnières* of 40 1866. In the five or six years which separate this landscape from the previous picture, however, he had discovered the assertive palette-knife technique, which is here employed to lend gravity and emphasis to an otherwise ordinary scene. (It was exactly this unorthodox technique, 'done with a spatula', that led even the artist's close friend Guillemet to ridicule his landscapes of this period as being unworthy of any museum.) Executed in a range of greys, browns, and dull greens, which vividly evoke the cloudy weather and low-lying sky, the picture recalls a passage in Cézanne's letters which reveals his growing concern to capture the most commonplace effects in nature. 'You are perfectly right to speak of grey', he confessed to Pissarro in October 1866, 'for grey alone reigns in nature, but it is terrifyingly hard to catch.' Scarcely less mundane are the telegraph wires and diminutive figures that inhabit this unprepossessing scene. The latter are unique in Cézanne's landscape art in revealing his momentary concern with the role of man in nature. Otherwise even the earliest

53

41 *Avenue at the Jas de Bouffan, c.* 1869

landscapes by the artist appear devoid of a sense of place or human intrusion, as though Cézanne was already seeking a more remote and impersonal vision of nature.

The compositional discipline implicit in the *View of Bonnières*, with its centrally placed church steeple and framing hills, is boldly asserted in the *Avenue at the Jas de Bouffan* of *c.* 1869. In this, the horizontals of the land and the verticals of the trees are linked by the diagonals of the foliage and pathway in an attempt to impose a simple geometric schema upon the most entrancing of scenes. Undeterred by the dappled light playing through the trees or the familiarity of the setting, Cézanne renders this theme with a concentration and insistence calculated to wring the strictest formal logic out of wayward nature.

This tendency culminates in the *Railway Cutting* of 1869–70, the most considered landscape of Cézanne's early years. Measuring more

41

35

54

than four feet (1.2 metres) across, this canvas shows the view over the garden wall of the Jas de Bouffan, with the Mont Sainte-Victoire – the dominant landmark of the countryside around Aix – visible at the right. Bounded below by two horizontal strips of land, which permit no entry into the scene, the picture is rigorously divided into three equal sections centred around the prominent railway cutting and signal-box. This strict, ternary design is reinforced by the heavy application of bold, localized hues and the rhyming curves of the hill, cutting, and mountain, which mark the broad divisions of the landscape.

So decisive a composition, on so grand a scale, can only have evolved after careful planning and may even have been painted in the studio, far removed from the disorderly world of nature. Further evidence of this is the existence of a preliminary drawing (Ch. 120) and oil sketch (V. 42) for the picture, the first such works to be encountered in Cézanne's landscape career. These reveal him gradually evolving the monumental construction of the final canvas by stripping away all that is extraneous to his chosen scheme. Thus, only from a photograph of the motif can one discover that the *36* prominent verticals lining both sides of the cutting are not fence posts but the irregular trunks of trees! In his determination to summon all his efforts to the creation of a masterpiece, Cézanne appears here – as in the *Still Life with a Black Clock* or the *Overture to Tannhäuser* – to transcend the furious passions of his youth and suddenly gain a measure of his future strength.

It is hard to think of an earlier landscape of comparable size and ambition that is so unburdened of pictorial fact or so condensed in expression. Yet, if this achievement already heralds the power and profundity of Cézanne's mature art, it lacks one ingredient which was to put that art in closer touch with nature – namely, the diverse sensations of seeing. Under the guidance of Pissarro and his fellow Impressionists, these were to form the basis of Cézanne's investigations in the immediately following years.

CHAPTER THREE

The Reluctant Impressionist (1871–1877)

Cézanne fled from Paris to Provence with the outbreak of the Franco-Prussian War in the summer of 1870. Apparently seeking to avoid conscription, he stopped briefly at Aix before settling with Hortense Fiquet in the town of l'Estaque, thirty kilometres south of Aix, in a house owned by his mother. There he worked for the remainder of the year, safely out of sight of his father, who remained ignorant of his liaison with Hortense. Soon after the armistice, in January 1871, he left l'Estaque, returning to Paris in the spring of that year, where he was reunited with Zola. Though the letters exchanged between them during this period no longer survive, Cézanne's paintings of these years indicate that he had reached a turning-point in his development.

42 *Melting Snow at l'Estaque*, 1870–71

43 *Still Life with Pot,
Bottle, Cup, and Fruit,
c.* 1871

Melting Snow at l'Estaque of 1870–71 illustrates the decisive changes   *42*
that had occurred in Cézanne's landscape art since the *Railway*   *35*
Cutting. Though still executed with the bold and dramatic contrasts of
colour and the sweeping brushstrokes of the artist's earlier landscapes,
the picture shows a radical departure from them in two important
ways: firstly, it is a seasonal landscape and, secondly, a decidedly
imbalanced one. Focusing upon the precipitous diagonal of the snow-
covered hill at the left, Cézanne daringly balances this by the
vehemently applied browns and reds of the landscape and houses
beyond. The result is a dynamic equilibrium very different from the
static, symmetrical composition of the *Railway Cutting.* (A similarly
precipitous composition, done in the same style in Paris early in 1872,
is V. 56.) When taken together with the fact that Cézanne here
chooses to portray a specific time of year, these changes reveal a new-
found desire to explore accidental effects in nature, as if in repudiation
of the strictures and certainties of his landscapes of the immediately
preceding years.

A similar freedom is apparent in Cézanne's portraits and still lifes of
this period. In a remarkably sympathetic portrait of Valabrègue, for   *44*
instance, the uncommunicative figure of the picture of 1866 now   *19*
appears as a tender and submissive one, his head inclined and his
features pensive, stressing the creative nature of his temperament. No
less felicitous in its way is a *Still Life with Pot, Bottle, Cup, and Fruit,*   *43*

which departs from the rigid symmetry of the *Still Life with a Black Clock* in favour of an unequal distribution of masses akin to that of *Melting Snow at l'Estaque*. In works such as these Cézanne appears to be challenging himself to find order and harmony in a seemingly casual grouping of pictorial elements. To be sure, his first steps in this direction are somewhat tentative. Witness the way in which he employs the shadow of the bottle in the *Still Life* to add an almost illicit symmetry to the composition. But this cannot detract from the fact that the artist was gradually abandoning the wilfully contrived compositional schemes of the *Black Clock* or the *Railway Cutting* in favour of those which appeared more true to life.

These tendencies were to develop rapidly as a result of the next decisive move in Cézanne's career. Resettled in Paris late in 1871, the artist's only child Paul was born there on 4 January 1872. Shortly afterwards Cézanne was visited by Achille Emperaire, who found him as irritable and uneasy as ever, living in noisy accommodation and (once again) having abandoned all his friends. Seeking the more congenial surroundings of the countryside, and realizing that he could no longer work in Provence, where Hortense and the infant Paul might be discovered by his father, Cézanne moved to the village of Pontoise, outside Paris, in the autumn of 1872. His decision was prompted by the fact that Pissarro resided there and had already succeeded in gathering around him a group of painters, his old friend Guillaumin among them, who shared Cézanne's dedication to working outdoors.

That this move was almost immediately beneficial for Cézanne's art is apparent from a letter by Pissarro to the painter Guillemet, dated September 1872, which declares: 'Our friend, Cézanne, raises our expectations, and I have seen and have at home a painting of remarkable vigour and power. If, as I hope, he stays some time in Auvers, where he is going to live, he will astonish a lot of artists who were too hasty in condemning him.' Ever generous and encouraging to those less confident than himself, Pissarro here reveals those qualities that were to make him the patriarchal leader – and greatest teacher – among the Impressionists. He also divulges Cézanne's plan of settling in Auvers, a village outside Pontoise, where the artist moved late in 1872 or early the following year. There he took up residence near the eccentric country doctor, Paul Gachet, an amateur artist and avid admirer and collector of the new group of painters, Pissarro among them. Gachet was also the proud owner of a printing press on which he encouraged both Pissarro and Cézanne to make a

44 *Portrait of Antony Valabrègue, c.* 1871

number of etchings during these years. Before long, Gachet had also become the first collector of Cézanne's pictures, otherwise exchangeable at this time only to pay the artist's grocery bills. Good-natured and charitable to so many struggling artists of his day, it was Gachet who tended Van Gogh at Auvers before his suicide in July 1890.

Cézanne and his family remained at Auvers until spring 1874. The works which he produced there indicate that this was among the most contented – and collaborative – moments of the artist's career. Painting alongside Pissarro, and in close association with Guillaumin, Cézanne appears to have dropped his guard in order to contribute to the creative life of the group. Photographs of the period show him in the countryside with Pissarro or striding out on his own in search of a landscape motif, protected from the sun's rays by a broad-brimmed hat. Drawings show Dr Gachet instructing Cézanne in the art of

46

45 *Self-Portrait, c.* 1873

46 Photograph of Cézanne at Auvers, *c.* 1873

47 *Dr Gachet and Cézanne etching, c.* 1873

48 (right) *Portrait of Pissarro, c.* 1873

49 (far right) Camille Pissarro, *Portrait of Paul Cézanne,* 1874

etching; and Cézanne also made several drawings of Pissarro   47, 48
(Ch. 298–301) and one etching of Guillaumin during these years. As if
further to declare his solidarity with his companions, he included a
landscape by Guillaumin in the back of a *Self-Portrait* of c. 1873.   45
Dressed in rugged outdoor clothing and sporting an unruly mane of
hair and beard, Cézanne here bears an alert and inquisitive expression
which testifies to his more approachable – if still unashamedly
uncouth – manner. Similarly, Pissarro's depictions of the artist show
an imposing but affectionate personality, friend not only to Pissarro   49
but to his rapidly expanding family. But the most revealing evidence
of the liberating and congenial atmosphere in which Cézanne worked
at Auvers are drawings such as *Family in a Garden*, which depicts a   50
relaxed outdoor gathering among friends, possibly at the house of Dr
Gachet, who is portrayed in a separate study at the upper right of
the sheet. To this may be added a small canvas, *Painter at Work*,   51
executed with a freedom and spontaneity that testify to the artist's
uninhibited powers of expression during these brief Impressionist
years.

Cézanne's *Painter at Work* also reveals the major changes which had
taken place in his art under Pissarro's guidance. Encouraged by the

50 *Family in a Garden*, c.1873

latter to become more attentive to the delicate gradations of light and atmosphere to be found in nature, Cézanne widened his palette and varied his brushstroke to represent the flickering effects of light and colour he observed before him. Though the earliest works executed in this manner lack the concentration and authority of the *Avenue at the Jas de Bouffan* or the *Railway Cutting*, they betray a new-found humility before nature which was eventually to permit Cézanne to record his sensations of landscape with an unparalleled richness of tone and hue.

Cézanne's first steps towards this goal are a series of views of the road through Auvers which led to Dr Gachet's house. In the majority

41,35

51 *Painter at Work*, c. 1873

of these, the trees are bare and the colours limited to dull greys and browns, suggesting that they were painted in the winter of 1872–73. Pissarro also executed a number of comparable works during this period. But these invariably include human figures and a greater wealth of naturalistic detail than Cézanne's stark scenes. In what is perhaps the finest of them, the artist centres the composition upon a   52 solitary tree growing beside the Gachet family residence and balances this by the converging diagonals of the road on either side. Most characteristic of all, however, is his tendency to permit the road to rise up the picture, rather than truly recede – a device that brings the middle distance forward and adds to the taut surface harmony of the design. Though the effect of this is somewhat claustrophobic, it suggests that Cézanne remained wary, even when painting such prosaic little scenes, of admitting any gaps into the composition that might weaken its overall unity.

These concerns appear accentuated in the artist's most impressive landscape of this period, the so-called *House of the Hanged Man* of   53

1873–74. In this Cézanne focuses so closely upon a bend in a road, lined with houses and trees, that the entire composition appears 'walled-up' and impregnable. Centred around the converging lines of the road at the left and the cottage at the right, the space between these is filled by the landscape in the middle distance, which rises to a high horizon surmounted by clear, blue sky. Even the latter affords little relief from the oppressive feel of the whole, so densely and evenly has the artist coated every inch of his canvas with paint. Executed in part with a palette knife, the picture is encrusted with thick, overlaid touches of colour which surpass anything to be found in Pissarro's art of these years. Though the varied application of paint and the subtle nuances of light and hue betray Cézanne's greater receptivity to nature, the insistent force of the handling reveals that there was one thing the artist was unwilling to sacrifice to the demands of greater illusionism: namely, the material reality of the surface he was creating.

52 *The House of Dr Gachet, c.* 1873

53 *The House of the Hanged Man*, 1873–74

The House of the Hanged Man was one of three works by Cézanne
exhibited at the first Impressionist exhibition of 1874, one of the
landmarks in the history of early modern art. Organized in opposition
to the official Salon, with its conservative jury and predictable
honours, the exhibition opened two weeks before the Salon, on 15
April, and ran for one month. It was held in the former studios of the
photographer Nadar on the Boulevard des Capucines and consisted of
over 160 works by thirty artists, who, for the price of a small
membership fee, were entitled to exhibit any works of their choice
without submitting these to an officiating jury. Among the artists
included were Boudin, Cézanne, Degas, Guillaumin, Monet, Berthe
Morisot, Pissarro, Renoir, and Sisley. (Manet alone refused to exhibit

with the new insurgents, preferring instead the sanction of the official Salon.) Though the group called itself the *Société anonyme des artistes, peintres, sculpteurs, graveurs, etc.*, in recognition of its democratic foundations, soon after the exhibition opened the critic Louis Leroy dubbed them 'Impressionists', taking this name from one of Monet's exhibited canvases – *Impression, Sunrise*. Intended as a term of abuse, this title was defiantly adopted by the group itself and has since become synonymous with all that is most appealing in late nineteenth-century French painting.

With its emphasis upon bright colours, summary brushwork, and contemporary subject matter, the exhibition caused a sensation among public and critics alike, schooled on the smooth finish and more 'elevated' themes of the annual Salon. Not all of this criticism was hostile, however, with the writer Armand Silvestre in particular finding much to admire in the works of Monet, Pissarro, and Sisley. Cézanne, on the other hand, fared less well. 'Shall we mention Cézanne who, by the way, has his own legend?', wrote the critic of *Le Rappel*. 'No known jury has ever, even in its dreams, imagined the possibility of accepting a single work by this painter, who came to the Salon carrying his paintings on his back, like Jesus Christ carrying the cross. An over-exclusive love of yellow has compromised Cézanne's future up to now.' This 'love of yellow' presumably refers to the preponderance of that colour in the *House of the Hanged Man* and probably also in Cézanne's other exhibited landscape, an unidentified *Landscape at Auvers*. At least one visitor to the exhibition, however, found that yellow much to his liking. He was Count Doria, a wealthy financier and collector of contemporary painting, who purchased the *House of the Hanged Man* shortly after the exhibition closed – a rare mark of commendation for an otherwise maligned painter.

Cézanne's third entry to the 1874 exhibition was his *Modern Olympia*, which took its name from the famous canvas by Manet that had created such a scandal at the Salon of 1865. A self-declared admirer of Manet's work, Cézanne had already painted an earlier variation on it in *c*. 1869 (V. 106). Though freer in handling and more highly keyed in colour, the later version is similar in conception and portrays the seated figure of the artist observing a reclining female nude attended by a negro servant. Of all the works shown at the first Impressionist exhibition, this aroused the most hostile criticism. 'On Sunday the public saw fit to sneer at a fantastic figure that is revealed under an opium sky to a drug addict', wrote one reviewer. 'This apparition of a little pink and nude flesh, which is being pushed, in the

54

54 *A Modern Olympia, c.* 1873

empyrean cloud, by a kind of demon or incubus, like a voluptuous
vision, this corner of artificial paradise, has suffocated the most
courageous, and M. Cézanne merely gives the impression of being a
sort of madman who paints in delirium tremens.'

Much has been written about Cézanne's intentions in his *Modern
Olympia*. Was the picture conceived as a homage to Manet's canvas –
or as a parody of it? Considering its small size, sketchy handling, and
substitution of Manet's insolent courtesan by an ungainly, almost ape-
like nude, it is hard to imagine that the picture was conceived in a
wholly reverential manner. More important is the figure of the artist
himself, included in the guise of a client at the right of the scene. We
have already noted how frequently Cézanne introduced himself into
his early subject pictures in the role of dreamer, would-be lover, or

55 *The Picnic, c.* 1874

even voyeur. Only the young Rembrandt insinuated himself more often into his own imaginary compositions, as if to lend to them a stamp of authenticity. But if Rembrandt introduces himself in the role of eyewitness, to give added veracity to the scene, Cézanne appears instead to sublimate his own hidden desires through his various pictorial disguises, as though this is the only acceptable way of channelling their release.

A Modern Olympia is among the last of the artist's works to include such a thinly disguised self-portrait, face to face with the object of his desires. Moreover, it is one of Cézanne's last overt explorations of the theme of female sexuality. For, although the artist was to return to the subject of the *Temptation of St Anthony* in the mid-1870s (V. 240 & 241; RWC 40 & 41; Ch. 445–453) and explore the related themes of *Bathsheba* (V. 252, 253, & 255) and the *Eternal Feminine* (V. 247; RWC

68

56 *An Afternoon in Naples*, 1876–77

57) during these same years, the majority of his multi-figure pictures
of 1870–77 portray bathers or people in contemporary dress relaxing   55
outdoors. Otherwise his chief preoccupation as a figure painter
during this period was a series of works in all media spanning the years
1866 to 1877 on the theme of *An Afternoon in Naples* or *The Rum
Punch*, an exotic title suggested by Guillemet. Probably also inspired
by Manet's *Olympia*, these are likewise concerned with the subject of
human eroticism. But whereas Cézanne's early explorations of this
theme (V. 112 & RWC 34) view it in a repellent light, his final
canvases (V. 223 & 224) see it in what (for Cézanne at least) appears a   56
more celebratory vein.

One month after the closure of the Impressionist exhibition,
Cézanne returned to Aix, his wife and son remaining in Paris. Hoping
for a long stay in Provence – 'where the views offer so many

opportunities for my painting' – he discovered upon his arrival that his reputation had preceded him and that the director of the Musée Granet, 'driven by a curiosity fed by the Paris papers, which mentioned the Cooperative [i.e. the newly formed Impressionist group], wished to see for himself how far the menace to painting went.' Since the director was still Joseph Gibert, Cézanne's early drawing master, the 'menace' was unlikely to please his former tutor. When informed by Cézanne that his own productions were as nothing compared with those of the 'big criminals of Paris', who replaced modelling by the study of tones in order to capture a more accurate impression of nature, Gibert closed his eyes and turned his back. (His response was mild. Gibert's successor forbade any of Cézanne's works from entering the Aix Museum until after his death, which occurred in 1926. By this time they were no longer affordable. Only in 1984 did the French State consign eight small canvases by the artist to the Musée Granet, at last according Cézanne official recognition in his native city.)

In the autumn of 1874 Cézanne returned to Paris. Though little is known of his activities during the following year, it seems likely that he continued to paint outdoors in the countryside around the French capital in an attempt to accommodate the lessons of Impressionism to his own desire for a more structured and synthetic pictorial style. The seriousness and circumspection with which Cézanne oversaw his own creative development during these years is evident in a number of ways. Not only did he repeatedly return to painting the same scenes, such as the road at Auvers, until he had given them definitive expression, but he signed many of his canvases and, in 1873, even dated two of them (V. 138 & 139) – a unique instance in Cézanne's career and one which testifies to his desire to document this turning-point in his development. Finally, in September 1874 he wrote reassuringly to his mother from Paris of his increased confidence in his creative powers: 'I am beginning to consider myself stronger than all those around me, and you know that the good opinion I have of myself has only been reached after serious consideration. I have to work all the time, not to reach that final perfection which earns the admiration of imbeciles . . . I must strive after perfection only for the satisfaction of becoming truer and wiser.'

Cézanne's landscapes of the mid-1870s testify to his desire to 'strive after perfection' even when confronting imperfect nature. In one of the most Impressionist of them, a *View of Auvers* of 1873–74, the artist adopts a light palette of pinks, whites, blues, yellows, and greens, to

57

57 *View of Auvers*, 1873–74

portray a hillside site of houses and trees in a mixed technique of daubs and patches of colour which vividly evoke the play of sunlight over the scene. Framed below by a fence and road and, on either side, by groups of trees, the structure of this picture appears otherwise undermined by the loose and unblended touches of colour and the variegated range of hues. These make it one of the most insubstantial – if entrancing – of the artist's Impressionist views.

Within a year or two of completing this picture Cézanne painted *The Road* or *The Wall*. In this the brushwork appears more orderly and regulated and the divisions of the composition more clearly defined, with the erect verticals of the trees framing a distant view of houses and hills that is itself carefully structured to lend order and harmony to the composition. Even more revealingly, in 1875–77 Cézanne painted a rare imaginary landscape along these same principles. This is *The Harvest*, a scene which derives its contemporary theme of rural labour from Pissarro but its consciously classical composition from Poussin. With its planar construction, clear framing elements, and finite spatial recession – not to mention the rhyming forms of the clouds and trees – *The Harvest* possesses a formal

58 *The Road*, or *The Wall*, *c.* 1875–76

59 *The Harvest*, 1875–77

logic and cohesion which provide a measure of Cézanne's own ideals in landscape painting, even when working from nature. Though *The Road* is inevitably more varied in colour and less systematic in handling, the fundamental similarities between these two pictures already reveal the extent to which Cézanne was seeking here (in his own, later words) 'to make of Impressionism something solid and durable, like the art of the museums.'

A graphic demonstration of Cézanne's antipathy towards the looseness and flimsiness of much Impressionist painting is his copy *61* after *The Seine at Bercy* by his friend, Guillaumin. Though identical in *60* size and largely faithful to the composition of the original, Cézanne's version introduces stronger contrasts of tone and colour in an effort to create a more decisive composition. Moreover, it enlarges the forms of the figures along the shore, the barges, and the distant bridge, again to add clear structural accents to the design. But perhaps the most revealing addition are the billowing clouds that Cézanne creates out of Guillaumin's atmospheric and undifferentiated sky. These provide a 'frame' for the elements below and serve to unite the upper and lower portions of the picture.

Cézanne chose not to exhibit with the Impressionists at their second group exhibition in 1876 and instead returned to Aix early that year, eventually settling for the summer in l'Estaque. There he painted the first view of what was to become one of his favourite landscape subjects, the magnificent panorama of the Gulf of Marseilles seen from the town, surmounted by the serene Mediterranean sky. 'It's like a playing-card. Red roofs over the blue sea', he exclaimed in a letter to Pissarro of July 1876, '. . . the vegetation doesn't change here. The olive and pine trees always keep their leaves. The sun here is so tremendous that it seems to me as if the objects were silhouetted not

60 Armand Guillaumin, *The Seine at Bercy*, 1873–75

61 *The Seine at Bercy* (after Guillaumin), *c.* 1877

only in black and white but in blue, red, brown and violet. I may be
mistaken, but this seems to me to be the opposite of modelling.'
Exhilarated by these striking contrasts of tone and hue, Cézanne
adopted a firm handling and carefully constructed composition for
this picture, which contrasts the diagonal slope of the land with the
horizontal band of the sea. Silhouetted against the intense blues of the
latter rise the houses and chimneys of the foreground, one of which
aligns itself with the distant hills, linking foreground with distance.

The emphatic application of paint in this *View of l'Estaque* also
occurs in two landscapes executed in Pontoise, where Cézanne
returned in 1877. Both of these bear close connections with Pissarro,
with whom Cézanne worked during this year. *The Road at Pontoise* of 64
1875–77 portrays the same view as a canvas by Pissarro of 1875, 63
suggesting that both may have been painted on a joint excursion into
the countryside. Characteristically, Cézanne omits the anecdotal
figures of Pissarro's picture and views the scene at closer range,

62 *L'Estaque*, 1876

banking it up with a group of tall trees at the left and consistently stressing the internal cohesion of the composition. All of these changes – most of them omissions – convert Pissarro's engaging and inhabitable landscape into one of formidable austerity and single-minded concentration.

An even greater departure from Impressionist method is Cézanne's *L'Etang des Soeurs, Osny* of 1877 (V. 174), first owned by Pissarro. In this Cézanne reverts to his technique of the 1860s of applying paint with a palette knife to create a thick, weighty texture. But whereas his earlier works employ this technique unsystematically, in the canvas of 1877 he aligns his patches of colour parallel to one other and exploits the straight edges obtainable with the palette knife, as though seeking a greater uniformity of handling.

Inevitably, this search for a more systematic method of paint application was to prove easier for the artist when creating from the imagination, away from the multifarious sensations of nature. Thus it is in Cézanne's bather compositions of the mid–1870s that one

63 Camille Pissarro, *The Road at Pontoise*, 1875

64 *The Road at Pontoise*, 1875–77

65 *Three Female Bathers*, 1874–75

observes him first formulating a style which would eventually lead him out of the apparent illogicalities of Impressionism towards a more disciplined and decisive manner of painting. Most of these portray groups of male or female bathers and foreshadow what was to become one of the central concerns of Cézanne's later years – the creation of monumental figure paintings of the nude in a landscape setting in the manner of the Old Masters.

In what would appear to be his earliest explorations of this theme (V. 264 & 265) Cézanne portrays a sequence of figures in consciously diversified poses. As in his subject pictures of the 1860s, overlapping between the figures is studiously avoided; though, unlike those works, the bather compositions appear noticeably devoid of literary content or of the brooding emotionalism of Cézanne's early years. Instead, they reveal a prevailing concern to treat the human figure as an exercise in formal composition.

Conscious that the frieze-like disposition of the pictures of *c.* 1874 lacked both unity and focus, Cézanne soon evolved a compositional scheme for his female bather paintings which portrayed from three to five nude figures in a pyramidal arrangement, with a standing bather surrounded by seated or crouching figures on either side. A water-colour of this subject, done in preparation for a painting (V. 266), 65 depicts these bulky and somewhat graceless nudes in a landscape created out of diagonally aligned strokes of colour which move from lower left to upper right. As we shall see, this is the first intimation of an orderly and rhythmic manner of paint application that was to dominate Cézanne's art of the immediately following years.

Though fewer in number, Cézanne's male bather pictures of this period are more varied, inventive, and uninhibited in conception, as if the artist were still recalling in them his boyhood outings with Zola

66 *Bathers in Repose*, 1876–77

67 *Portrait of Victor Chocquet*, 1876–77

and Baille around Aix. In what is undoubtedly the finest of them – and, by far, the largest and most ambitious of Cézanne's figure paintings of the 1870s – the artist portrays four heroically posed nudes against a panoramic landscape dominated by the Mont Sainte-Victoire. In the statuesque attitudes of the figures and the harmonious relationship established between them and their surroundings, Cézanne attains a grandeur and solemnity of expression that already rivals the monumental figure painters of the past.

66

Nor did such qualities go unnoticed by certain of the artist's early critics; for at the third Impressionist exhibition in 1877, a study for the *Male Bathers* (V. 273) was singled out for praise by Georges Rivière. After noting that Cézanne had been the most attacked of all artists for the past fifteen years, Rivière observed: 'M. Cézanne is, in his works, a Greek of the great period; his canvases have the calm and heroic serenity of the paintings and terracottas of antiquity, and the ignorant who laugh at the *Bathers*, for example, impress me like Barbarians criticizing the Parthenon . . . M. Cézanne is a painter, and a great painter . . . His beautiful still lifes, so exact in the relationship of tones, have a solemn quality of truth. In all his paintings the artist produces emotion because he himself experiences in the face of nature a violent emotion that his craftsmanship transmits to the canvas.'

Cézanne showed seventeen works at this exhibition (including ill. 62), the majority of them loaned by Victor Chocquet, a retired customs official who owned an important collection of works by Delacroix and Renoir. When, in 1875, the latter introduced him to Cézanne, Chocquet became an avid admirer and collector of this artist's work. At the exhibition of 1877 he tirelessly championed the cause of Cézanne, whom (according to one critic) 'he placed on the highest level'. However, the same critic concludes: 'Many were amused by Chocquet's enthusiasm, which they considered something like a gentle insanity.'

Though Cézanne exhibited works drawn from the entire range of his art and was accorded a prime site in the display, he still drew little favourable response from the critics. To be sure, his old friend Zola commended him as 'certainly the greatest colourist of the group' and added: 'There are, in the exhibition, some Provençal landscapes of his that have a splendid character. The canvases of this painter, so strong and so deeply felt, may cause the bourgeois to smile, but they nevertheless contain the makings of a great artist.' But the majority of critics and public found Cézanne's art incomprehensible, even dangerous to one's health.

68 *Dahlias, c.* 1873

67   Much of their abuse was directed at a portrait of Chocquet, described by one dissenting critic as resembling a notorious murderer of the day rendered in tones of chocolate. In fact, the picture is among Cézanne's noblest and most penetrating characterizations. Executed with bold, agitated strokes of thick paint, it superbly evokes the nervous energy and introspection of the lively and cultivated Chocquet.

    Cézanne also exhibited three still lifes and three flower-pieces at the third Impressionist exhibition, including among the latter one watercolour. Though his dedication to working outdoors had left him with little time for such pictures during the early 1870s, following Pissarro's example Cézanne executed a handful of flower-

68   pieces around 1873. One of the simplest and most successful of these depicts a vase owned by Dr Gachet, also included in a flower-piece by

69 *Still Life with Apples*, 1873–77

Pissarro of *c*. 1870. But Cézanne's favourite still-life subjects of the
mid-1870s were small groups of apples studied at close range and   69
painted with all the variety and intensity of colour that characterized
his more complex encounters with landscape.

Contemporary with these is a small group of more ambitious still
lives which move increasingly to explore the formal and colouristic
affinities between a variety of inanimate objects seen against a
patterned background, a development which culminates in the *Still
Life with Compotier* of *c*. 1880. One of the first of these, *The Dessert* of   6, 70
c. 1877, presents a cut-glass carafe, glass, and fruit on an elaborate
Louis XV commode. Set against a plain ochre background, these
objects are portrayed with a sobriety and simplicity that belie their
rarefied nature. Adding to the pervasive calm of the work are the
light, even tonality and brighter colour of Cézanne's art of the mid-
1870s, so different from the dramatic contrasts of his still lifes of the
preceding decade. Yet another advance over these early pictures is a
sense of clear spatial intervals – or caesuras – in the composition,
which endow the objects with a monumental dignity.

70 *The Dessert, c.* 1877

71   Another work of this period depicts a soup tureen, bottle, and basket of apples against a background of painted canvases, including (at the left) a landscape by Pissarro, in whose house Cézanne reputedly executed this picture in 1877. Aligning the straight lines of the tureen and bottle with those of the landscape above, Cézanne contrasts these against the swelling curves of the basket and apples, themselves echoed in the unidentified painting of fowl which hangs in the centre of the picture. This approach appears more fully developed in a third work of these years in which a vase, cup, apples, and napkin are seen

72   against a geometrically patterned wallpaper. Arranged in a descending diagonal line, like *The Dessert*, the objects in this picture appear even more closely integrated with their surroundings through the complex play of diagonals which converge upon them from above. These in turn are mirrored in the disposition of the napkin, which fans

84

71 *Still Life with Soup Tureen, c.* 1877

out in two ascending lines to encompass all the still-life objects and relate them to the rhythms of the wallpaper, like a ground bass line supporting a more animated melody.

The decorative devices of these pictures recur in two of Cézanne's most remarkable portraits of *c.* 1877. In *Chocquet seated,* the artist *73* portrays his friend and champion in an interior furnished with a desk, paintings, and patterned carpet, whose rectilinear lines dominate the composition. This is organized in a patchwork construction of intersecting verticals and horizontals which link all points in space to the flat surface of the canvas. Enhancing this effect are the inlaid touches of colour out of which Cézanne has built the picture. The majority of these are square or rectangular in shape and so densely fitted together that they resemble marquetry, or even mosaic. Further unifying the composition is the firmly planted Chocquet, whose

72 *Still Life, c.* 1877

frontal pose, straight back, and carefully crossed legs align themselves with the two main axes of the picture and whose interlocking fingers provide the key to the tightly meshed construction of the whole.

74   Closely related to this is Cézanne's masterly portrait of his wife seated in a red armchair, a picture that moved the German poet Rilke to write some of his most eloquent passages on painting. Posed squarely and frontally before the viewer, Madame Cézanne is portrayed leaning to the left, revealing the broad back of the chair on the opposite side which effectively stabilizes the composition. This stability is attained not simply by a balanced distribution of masses but by the permeation of the entire canvas by intense, saturated colour, most especially the blues and reds of the dress and chair. Far from being confined to these objects, modified touches of these two basic

73 *Chocquet seated, c.* 1877

hues infiltrate all portions of the picture and combine breathtakingly to build up the form of Madame Cézanne's head. '*It's as if every place were aware of all the other places*', exclaimed Rilke in an attempt to convey the pulsating vitality of Cézanne's approach to colour in this picture. Adding to the overall harmony of the effect is the decorative patterning on the wallpaper behind, which echoes the axes of the sitter's face, pose, and costume, and looms forward at the lower left to declare its affinity with the tassel of the chair. This device is reminiscent of the decorative links employed by Cézanne in the *Overture to Tannhäuser* of *c.* 1869–70. In the nearly ten years which separate these pictures, however, the artist had discovered an additional means of achieving overall harmony in his pictures. This was through the mutual interaction of colours. First revealed to him in the countryside of Pontoise and Auvers, this proved to be the greatest legacy of Cézanne's Impressionist years.

33

74 Madame Cézanne in a Red Armchair, c. 1877

CHAPTER FOUR

The Instinctive Classicist (1878–1885)

As he approached his fortieth birthday, Cézanne had cause to reflect on his lack of worldly achievement compared with those of his immediate circle. In 1878, his close friend Zola had scored his first great success with *L'Assommoir*, the latest of his Rougon-Macquart series of novels. Begun in 1871 and concluded in 1893, this would eventually comprise twenty volumes tracing the history of a single family during the Second Empire – many of them inspired by Zola's boyhood in Aix. Two years earlier, Monet had sold a major canvas for two thousand francs, or roughly seven times the valuation that would be placed on a single Cézanne in the months after his death. Renoir, too, was enjoying unprecedented success with a series of important portrait commissions, the most notable of which portrayed the wife of Zola's publisher, Madame Charpentier and her children (Metropolitan Museum of Art, New York). Exhibited to great acclaim at the Salon of 1879, this picture earned the artist one thousand francs and temporarily led him to abandon the Impressionist cause and choose to exhibit at the Salon again the following year. Even Pissarro managed to sell a number of works at reasonable prices during these years and could now count among his collectors Caillebotte, Chocquet, de Bellio, Dubourg, and the young Paul Gauguin.

In contrast, Cézanne had few champions beside Chocquet and the paint merchant and picture dealer, Père Tanguy. Though far from wealthy, the latter was a generous supporter of the new painters, regularly supplying them with materials in exchange for pictures, despite the fact that he stood little chance of selling these. In the late 1880s, Tanguy was to perform this service for the struggling Van Gogh, whose two portraits of him reveal the warmth, humility, and ebullience of this squat little man, who energetically championed the cause of the Impressionists. Already in March 1878 Cézanne owed Tanguy more than two thousand francs for painting materials. By 1885 this sum was still unpaid and the artist's debt had more than doubled. In return, all the kind-hearted colour merchant received were Cézanne's unsaleable canvases. Until Tanguy's death in 1893, his dark little premises on the rue Clauzel was the only place in Paris where Cézanne's pictures could be seen.

Cézanne's precarious financial state took a further turn for the worse early in 1878, when his father intercepted a letter to him from Chocquet revealing the existence of Madame Cézanne and young Paul. Irate at this affront to family morals – and conveniently overlooking the fact that two of his own children had been born out of wedlock – Louis-Auguste reduced his son's financial allowance by half, whereupon Cézanne was forced to beg Zola to lend him the necessary funds to support his wife and son. This crisis, which lasted until the autumn of 1878, can only have been deeply humiliating for the painter, scorned by his aging father and forced to rely on the generosity of his increasingly affluent boyhood friend. As late as December of that year Cézanne confessed to Zola that the lack of understanding between himself and his father had left him 'more disturbed than ever'.

Cézanne spent much of 1878 in Provence, dividing his time between Aix and l'Estaque. His memory still fresh from the critical condemnation that had greeted his submissions to the third Impressionist exhibition the year before, he met with comparable abuse in his native town, where even the local schoolboys reviled him. Again rejected at the annual Salon, he confessed to Zola in a letter of April 1878: 'I am working; poor results and too far removed from the general understanding.' It was doubtless this combination of critical disdain and severe self-doubt that led him to refuse to exhibit at the fourth Impressionist exhibition in 1879. Instead, he submitted once more to the Salon, which accepted works by Monet and Renoir but rejected him and Sisley.

If Cézanne was still struggling to gain a measure of critical and commercial success, his friend Zola had already arrived. In the summer of 1878, the novelist purchased a summer house and garden at Médan outside Paris. There he entertained an ever-widening circle of literary friends and acquaintances at animated *soirées* presided over by himself and Madame Zola. Though the increasingly reclusive Cézanne visited him there on a number of occasions between 1879 and 1885, he cannot have felt entirely at ease in such company or surroundings and later reputedly confessed that going to visit Zola, with his servants and fine carpets, was like 'paying a visit to a minister of state'.

75 *The Bridge at Maincy*, 1879

76 *Avenue at the Jas de Bouffan*, 1878–80

77 *Le Château de Médan*, c. 1880

78 Drawing for *Le Château de Médan*, c. 1880

The hiatus between Zola and Cézanne was further widened in 1880, when the novelist was requested by his friend to take up his pen in defence of the Impressionists. In that year, Monet and Renoir had again gained acceptance to the annual Salon; but their works were hung so badly as to be scarcely visible. Using Cézanne as an intermediary, both artists petitioned Zola to intervene on their behalf with (as Cézanne put it) a 'few words . . . showing up the importance of the Impressionists and the real interest they have aroused.'

Zola consented and, in June 1880, published four long articles in *Le Voltaire* entitled 'Naturalism in the Salon'. Though their tone was still approving of the group's fundamental aims, Zola did not conceal his own misgivings about their abilities to attain their desired goal:

> The real misfortune is that no artist of this group has achieved powerfully and definitely the new formula that, scattered through their works, they all offer. The formula is there, endlessly diffused; but in no place, among any of them, is it to be found applied by a master. They are all forerunners. The man of genius has not arisen. We can see what they intend and find them right, but we seek in vain the masterpiece that is to lay down the formula and make heads bow before it. This is why the battle of the Impressionists has not yet ended; they remain inferior to what they undertake; they stammer without being able to find the word.

Of Cézanne himself Zola wrote only: 'Monsieur Paul Cézanne has the temperament of a great painter who still struggles with problems of technique, and remains closest to Courbet and Delacroix.' Though Cézanne could no longer be considered part of the Impressionist group and was never again to exhibit with them, Zola's words cannot have comforted him. To be sure, Cézanne had confessed to Zola only one year before: 'I am still striving to discover my way as a painter. Nature presents me with the greatest difficulties.' But it was one thing to admit this privately to one's closest friend and another to find that friend expressing similar doubts in public.

The 'difficulties' Cézanne refers to are evident in his landscapes of this period and in certain passages in his letters relating to them. In one of these Cézanne admits that the goal of his art should be 'the rendering of nature'. In another he writes to Zola from l'Estaque: 'As you say, there are some very beautiful views here. The difficulty is to reproduce them, this isn't exactly my line. I began to see nature rather late, though this does not prevent it being full of interest for me.' From these words it is clear that Cézanne sought to render the multifarious sensations that nature unfolded to his senses as truthfully as possible.

In a third letter of this period the artist describes an outing to Marseilles with his former drawing master, Gibert. This resulted in a disagreement about a suitable landscape subject which outlines the dilemma Cézanne himself faced when working from nature. 'When I went to Marseilles I was in the company of Monsieur Gibert', the artist recalls. 'These people see correctly, but they have the eyes of Professors. Where the train passes close to Alexis's country house, a stunning motif appears on the East side: Ste Victoire and the rocks that dominate Beaurecueil. I said: "What a lovely motif"; he replied: "The lines are too well balanced."'

From this it may be gleaned that, whereas the professorial Gibert preferred a more picturesque and informal arrangement of natural elements, Cézanne sought one which was inherently balanced and ordered – and equated beauty with a certain formality in nature. When one combines these remarks by the artist it is apparent that the chief challenge he set himself before a landscape subject was the seemingly contradictory one of portraying both nature's underlying order and its infinite variety.

The Bridge at Maincy of 1879 shows the artist grappling with these two concerns at a critical moment of his career. The scene chosen – that of a secluded footbridge framed by water and trees – is one that would have delighted Monet or Pissarro through its unpretentious charm and delicate gradations of light and hue. Though Cézanne, too, remains sensitive to these, he is equally concerned to discover a structural logic in this atmospheric and confusing scene. Setting the bridge squarely in the centre of the picture, and employing its two prominent arches as framing elements, he then proceeds to align the foreground trees with the bridge itself – not least by making the reflection of the arch at the left so distinct that it presses forward to link these two spatial planes. Enhancing this underlying symmetry are the changing hues of the water, which appears deep green in the centre and russet brown to either side. In his treatment of the foliage above, however, Cézanne employs a modulated range of emerald greens and whites in mosaic-like touches which evoke the play of dappled light over this enchanting scene and reveal the extent of his debt to his Impressionist years. The result is a picture which combines the richness of interest Cézanne experienced before nature and the 'well balanced' lines disapproved of by Gibert. Put another way, it is a kind of Impressionism made classical – one which possesses the authority of

75

79 *Self-Portrait*, *c*. 1880

the art of the Old Masters and the optical concerns of Cézanne's own generation.

One means of recording his sensations directly from nature which the artist increasingly employed during the late 1870s was watercolour. Cézanne had worked in watercolour from the start of his career and, as early as 1866, acknowledged the relative ease with which it could be handled when compared with oils. Only in his early maturity, however, did he begin to explore the unparalleled freedom and immediacy obtainable in this medium. In this he had few predecessors among French artists, though Delacroix had occasionally made watercolours and Granet had employed it regularly for some of his most atmospheric and inventive landscape studies. But neither of these masters accorded it a central place in his achievement. Cézanne, on the other hand, was eventually to produce nearly 650 watercolours – a number rivalling his output of just over 850 paintings. Moreover, with the sole exception of Turner – whose watercolours he is unlikely to have known – no artist of comparable stature has ever employed watercolour to further his researches in painting to a greater extent than Cézanne, who appears to have regarded his watercolours as comparable in importance to his oils and who is arguably the greatest of all masters of this notoriously difficult medium.

Watercolour had numerous advantages for Cézanne. For one, it enabled him to work quickly and freely and encouraged a less laboured approach to painting than oil. This (as we know from the artist himself) often afforded him a welcome release from his weightier researches in oil and is apparent in the spontaneity and exuberance of many of his watercolours. In addition, the transparency of the medium, in which delicate unblended strokes of colour appear to float over the surface of the paper, permitted him to achieve an unparalleled luminosity in these works. It also made possible an effect for which Cézanne constantly strove in his oils. With the white of the paper showing through, it allowed him to achieve those continuous colour modulations and rhythmical harmonies which proved more difficult in the opaque medium of oil. For in watercolour the unity of the entire work was in a sense 'assured' by the underlying whiteness of the paper.

The ease and confidence with which Cézanne handled watercolour and the frequency with which he employed it means that there is no consistent relationship between his works in this form and his paintings. In his early years, a number of watercolours are closely

80 *Hills with Houses and Trees*, 1880–83

connected with his more ambitious canvases and were presumably
done in preparation for them. Once he had begun to explore the
idiomatic possibilities of watercolour, however, Cézanne clearly
accorded it a more independent role in his creative thinking. Thus,
while some of his later watercolours may still have been conceived as
preparatory works, the majority find no direct counterpart among his
paintings. For this reason it is best to think of Cézanne's evolution as a
watercolourist as proceeding parallel to his development as a painter.
Though initially lagging behind the latter, his watercolour technique
eventually came to guide his experiments in painting, resulting in the
breathtaking freedom and luminosity of his very last works.

Generally speaking, Cézanne's watercolours of the late 1870s are
more cautious in handling, with touches of colour applied over a
carefully worked out under-drawing, as in the *Avenue at the Jas de
Bouffan* of 1878–80, where the artist returns to the motif of his earlier
canvas. Rather than viewing it from an oblique angle, which
permitted him to introduce strong diagonal accents into the
composition, Cézanne now places the avenue centrally on the sheet.
Rhythmically regulated by the intersecting verticals and horizontals

76
41

98

of the trees and land, the classical poise and symmetry of the design is enlivened by sparing touches of colour. In places these float freely over the surface of the paper; in others they are superimposed upon one another to achieve a faceted effect of delicate chromaticism which, even at this stage of Cézanne's career, appears lighter in touch and more nuanced in hue than anything to be seen in his paintings.

The geometric accents which dominate this composition are often to be found in Cézanne's landscape art of c. 1880, and suggest that the artist was wilfully seeking to introduce a mathematical rigour and precision into his pictures after the looser and less disciplined style of his Impressionist years. This may be seen in a remarkably revealing landscape drawing of 1880–83, in which the artist reinforced the vertical and horizontal lines of the trees and hills by employing a straight-edge to achieve a grid-like division of the sheet that anticipates Mondrian's near-abstract studies from nature of 1909–10. 80

These tendencies culminate in *Le Château de Médan*, probably of 1880. Painted from an island on the Seine, the picture was executed during a summer visit to Zola's country residence and shows the Château de Médan at the right, with its blue roof and red dormer windows. (Zola's house is off the scene, to the right of the Château.) 77

Ample evidence exists to suggest that *Le Château de Médan* was among Cézanne's most carefully planned works and may even have been intended to disabuse Zola of the notion that the Impressionists had yet to say anything definitive in their paintings. In a letter from Cézanne to Zola of June 1880 – the very month in which the writer's criticisms of Impressionism had appeared – the artist announced his desire to paint a landscape on his next visit to Médan and added deferentially 'if you are not alarmed at the length of time I risk taking', as though already aware of how much thought he intended to devote to this picture. Moreover, at least two preparatory drawings (Ch. 786 & 787) and one watercolour (RWC 89) were made for the picture. One of the drawings depicts the kernel of the composition and already announces its prevailing geometry. The watercolour portrays the entire scene from a position further to the right – a viewpoint that Cézanne eventually rejected, presumably because it lacked the firm framing elements of the final painting. 78

Few works by the artist are as insistently logical as *Le Château de Médan*, in which all of nature is perceived as essentially rectilinear. Horizontally banded into five nearly equal areas of river, bank, buildings, hills, and sky, the design is subdivided vertically by a rhythmic screen of trees which is itself rigorously symmetrical. At the

81 *Portrait of Madame Cézanne*, 1879–82

82 *Madame Cézanne and Hydrangea*, c. 1885

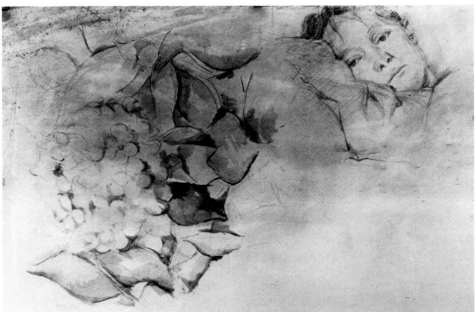

centre the darkened windows of two adjacent buildings frame a single tree and provide a fulcrum for the composition. But the stability of this scheme is far from lifeless. Densely binding all the forms of the landscape is a weft of diagonal brushstrokes of an unparalleled lustre and uniformity, which clothe nature's geometry in its ceaseless animation and enhance the richness and resolution of the work. This so-called 'constructive stroke' of c. 1880, with its uniform and directional application of paint, reveals Cézanne's desire to evolve a more systematic manner of handling after the mixed technique of his Impressionist years and endows the entire canvas with a tautly woven appearance. Possessed of such a high degree of decorative unity, it is little wonder that *Le Château de Médan* caught the eye of the young Gauguin, recently turned painter from an early career in the stock market, in whose collection this picture is first recorded.

Though less numerous than his landscapes, Cézanne's portraits of this period also reveal a desire for greater economy and monumentality in the presentation of a sitter and betray the increased confidence of his art during these years. The majority of them are portraits of himself and his family. In a well-known portrait of Madame Cézanne of c. 1879–82, the artist poses her in a mauve armchair against the floral-patterned wallpaper familiar from the *Still Life with Compotier*. Wearing a grey dress which echoes the colour of the background, Madame Cézanne stares out at the viewer, her mask-like features and dark, impenetrable eyes precluding any access to her thoughts. Such insights are, however, to be found in the more private medium of Cézanne's drawings, where his wife is occasionally shown daydreaming, dozing, or even sewing. And in a rare watercolour of Madame Cézanne, the artist portrays her alongside a delicate sprig of hydrangeas (in French, *hortensias*), an affectionate visual pun on the name of a woman who (whatever the limitations of their relationship) was a patient sitter for her husband and a devoted mother to his only son.

An even more frequent sitter for the artist was Paul *fils*. Given the boy's youthful and cantankerous nature – Cézanne refers to his son as 'terrible' in more than one letter of these years – it is inevitable that most of these studies are drawings, which chart every stage of the boy's development with that blind devotion that is peculiarly reserved for parents. Sleeping, reading, drawing, or smiling impishly for his father, Cézanne's son is portrayed with an affection and solicitude rarely encountered in the work of this most impersonal of painters. (Before the most doting of these, Rembrandt's portraits of

81
6

82

84

83 (left) *Portrait of the Artist's Son, c.* 1885

84 (above) *Portrait of the Artist's Son, c.* 1878

his son Titus come immediately to mind.) As he approached his early teens and was willing to pose for longer, Cézanne began to demand of him more formal sittings, such as those which resulted in the
83   disarming portrait of *c.* 1885. Posed proudly in a blue cap and jacket against a festively coloured background, the boy gazes out at the artist with a mischievous glance, as though assured of his father's love.

    Cézanne's self-portraits of the middle years encompass an even wider range of moods, from confidence to insecurity, anxiety to proud self-assertion. One of the most engaging of them shows the
79   artist against a lozenge-patterned background also visible in certain still lifes of this period. In this, the calm, meditative expression seems to arise as much from aesthetic considerations as from any self-assumed air. For, more than in any of his self-portraits, Cézanne here appears to be exploring the formal relationships between his own head and costume and the surrounding wallpaper. Thus, the artist's eyes, nose, beard and collar take on something of the zigzag lines and star-shaped forms of the background – a union of the organic and the geometric which culminates in the diamond-shaped form of the

85 *Self-Portrait, c.* 1883

86 (right) *Self-Portrait, c.* 1880

artist's right ear, which stands in for the lozenge motif in the
wallpaper at exactly the right point in the picture.

If such devices add an almost playful note to this portrait, the
absence of them from other works results in images of greater
solemnity. In certain of these, the artist confronts the viewer with an
expression of infinite wisdom and almost superhuman imperturba-   *1*
bility. (Here, too, one inevitably thinks of Rembrandt, who alone
among Cézanne's predecessors plumbed such hidden reserves of
human strength and will.) Drawings of the period, however, often
reveal a more vulnerable side of the artist's nature, at times   *85*
approaching a ghostly insubstantiality that cowers from the viewer's
gaze. Finally, in another self-portrait, Cézanne depicts himself
wearing the workaday clothes and humble expression of an ordinary   *86*
peasant. This is the Cézanne described by George Moore in his
Reminiscences as 'too rough, too savage a creature, [who] appeared in
Paris only rarely. We used to hear about him – he used to be met on
the outskirts of Paris wandering about the hillsides in jackboots. As no
one took the least interest in his pictures, he left them in the fields . . .'

Cézanne himself described this state even more succinctly in a letter to Zola of June 1878, when he characterized himself as 'an unhappy painter who has never been able to achieve anything . . .'

Deeply discouraged by the critical disapproval he had repeatedly experienced in Paris, Cézanne increasingly withdrew from the French capital during the early 1880s. In 1881 he returned to Pontoise to work with Pissarro. There he met Gauguin, who was receiving some instruction from Pissarro and tried to befriend Cézanne, only to be rebuffed by the ever-suspicious older master. Early in the next year, Renoir visited Cézanne in Aix and was warmly received, even being nursed through a bout of pneumonia by him. To the end of his life Cézanne was to show respect and admiration for Renoir's talents, so very different from his own – a respect which Renoir reciprocated by frequently returning to Provence to work alongside his friend. In 1880 Renoir also painted a pastel portrait of Cézanne, which reveals a warmth and humanity in the master, denied to us in his own self-portraits but willingly bestowed upon him by his kind-hearted friend.

In 1882, Cézanne also gained admission to the annual Salon through the generosity of another friend, Antoine Guillemet, by then a member of the jury. Taking advantage of a rule which permitted any such member to admit one work to the exhibition without official vetting, Guillemet allowed Cézanne – whom he listed as his pupil – to attain his long-standing ambition and exhibit a portrait that year. The work in question, an unidentified *Portrait of Monsieur L. A.* (Louis-Auguste Cézanne?), predictably drew little response from the critics. This effectively ended Cézanne's bid for official recognition in Paris, though he stubbornly continued to submit his canvases to the Salon jury for the next few years.

Other than his habitual sojourns in Paris and Provence, Cézanne and his family visited Renoir at La Roche-Guyon in the early summer of 1885. On his return to Aix in August that year, he passed briefly through Médan to see his friend Zola, now at work on his novel *L'Oeuvre*. Though both men were to live until the early years of this century, this proved to be the last meeting between them.

Although Cézanne's artistic output in the early 1880s was dominated by his achievements in landscape, he also continued to devote a significant proportion of his attention to figure paintings and (even more importantly) still life. Where the former was concerned, his interest remained with the theme of bathers, which he continued to explore in a number of works that have their origins in the compositional prototypes developed in the mid-1870s. Thus, the

87 *Three Female Bathers*, 1879–82

groups of female bathers typically employ a pyramidal arrangement around a standing central figure, the poses being devised to show contrasting views of the nude, in an effort to imbue these works with both grandeur and variety.

In one of the finest of these, Cézanne limits the group to three   87 figures, framed on either side by bending trees and further unified by the parallel brushstrokes familiar from these years. Through the simplicity of the arrangement and the vibrant colour and handling Cézanne achieves a gravity and intensity in this modestly sized canvas which heralds the great bather compositions of his final years. It also

88 *Five Male Bathers, c.* 1880

anticipates the bold and expressive distortions of the human figure of such later artists as Picasso and Matisse, the latter of whom purchased this picture while still a student in 1899. Thirty-seven years later, upon bequeathing it to the people of Paris, Matisse confessed: '. . . it has sustained me spiritually in the critical moments of my career . . . I have drawn from it my faith and my perseverance . . .'

If Cézanne's compositional 'type' for the theme of female bathers was the pyramid, his preferred scheme for their male counterparts was
88   the frieze. In a series of small canvases of *c.* 1879–85, the artist explored the theme of five or six male bathers seated, standing, or wading in the water. Seldom overlapping, and with their heads rising and falling across the canvas, these figures appear more closely interlinked than
66   the isolated and self-consciously statuesque bathers in the great Barnes canvas of *c.* 1877. The latter did, however, furnish the inspiration for

another group of works of these same years, which portray a single male bather seen against a distant landscape in heroic isolation – like the central figure in the Barnes picture. The grandest of them repeats 89 the pose of that figure, which is itself taken from a photograph of a standing male model that Cézanne owned. This may explain the powerful simplification of the contours which Cézanne employs in this work, as also the strength and harmony of the final composition. Welded to the forms and colours of the landscape, Cézanne's solitary bather assumes a grandeur and dignity arguably unobtainable through the study of the living model. In the equilibrium of his pose and the contemplative nature of his bearing, Cézanne appears to explore his own ideals for human existence – stable, self-contained, and at one with the world of nature.

Even more than in his imaginary bather pictures, Cézanne experienced his greatest creative independence when painting still life. Here alone was he able to preside over an arrangement of pictorial elements of little intrinsic significance and explore those formal and

89 *Great Male Bather,*
c. 1885

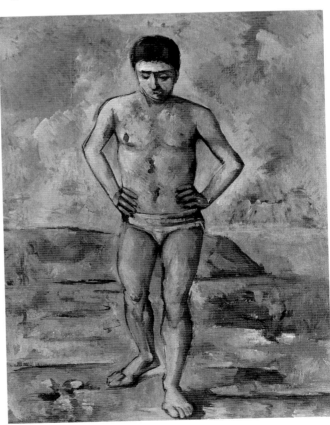

colouristic harmonies which constitute the essence of his art. In pursuing these, the artist enjoyed unparalleled artistic freedom; for, unlike his work in landscape, he exercised full control over the disposition of objects before him – that is to say, he could compose rather than merely select his motif. Acquaintances of Cézanne bear witness to the painstaking care he devoted to this preliminary stage in the planning. Thus, when Louis Le Bail observed the artist arranging a still life in the 1890s, he wrote: 'The cloth was very slightly draped upon the table, with innate taste. Then Cézanne arranged the fruits, contrasting the tones one against the other, making the complementaries vibrate, the greens against the reds, the yellows against the blues, tipping, turning, balancing the fruits as he wanted them to be, using coins of one or two sous for the purpose. He brought to this task the greatest care and many precautions; one guessed that it was a feast for the eye to him.'

Though Cézanne's remarkable inventiveness as a still-life painter almost never led him to repeat the identical arrangement of objects, two important canvases of the mid-1880s provide an exception to this rule and demonstrate the artist's powers of uncovering different relationships in the identical assemblage of ordinary things. Both of these portray a vase, jar, ginger pot and bowl of fruit resting on a table
90   draped with a napkin and seen against a chest of drawers. In one, the artist appears to have stood further away from the table when painting, thereby admitting to his field of vision an ornately decorated screen at the background left. No sooner has this asserted itself upon the scene than the other objects in the room declare their own rhythmic affinity with its lively patterning. The folds of the napkin become dynamic and animated, descending dramatically at the lower right as though in response to the screen on the opposite side. The handle of the ginger pot rises assertively; the key holes of the bureau loom forward; the plain-coloured vase acquires a marbled appearance; and the floral pattern on the jar in front of it is consciously stressed.

91   In another version of this composition, the virtual absence of the screen leads the artist to suppress all of these decorative features in favour of a grave and sober harmony – one which dispenses with the animated rhythms of the previous canvas and emphasizes instead the governing contours and plain surfaces of the forms. This is even apparent in the open drawer of the table in the foreground, which possesses a prominent handle and casts a deep shadow in one canvas but not in the other. In this comparison alone may be seen the subtlety

90 *Still Life on a Table*, 1883–87

91 *Still Life on a Table*, 1883–87

and selectivity of Cézanne's vision, which is constantly striving to uncover hidden affinities between disparate things in order to achieve the highest degree of formal integration in his pictures. Nor is it worth disputing which view of these objects is 'correct'. The truth is that both have been selected and scrutinized according to the needs of each picture. As a result the finished canvases possess an autonomy and integrity that no longer seek to imitate nature. As Cézanne declared in 1897: 'Art is a harmony which runs parallel with nature'.

93   Cézanne's ability to coax a seemingly infinite series of relationships out of the most modest arrangement of still-life objects reaches an undisputed peak in *The Blue Vase* of *c*. 1885. In this virtually every other element in the composition appears to respond to the centrally placed vase of flowers, whose intense blue saturates all parts of the canvas. At the left, the peeled tab of a wine bottle assumes the form of a petal; while, behind the vase, the scalloped contour of the plate echoes the left rim of the vase itself. Most remarkably of all, the spatial configuration of the scene mirrors the arrangement of the flowers in the vase, which rise vertically at the left and fan outwards at the opposite side. One of these even aligns itself with the edges of the wall, drawing this outermost area of the picture into the intricate network of relations which animate the composition. Sensitive, scrutinizing, and susceptible to the slightest opportunity to adjust one form to the requirements of another, Cézanne even depresses the bulge and base of the vase at the right. This permits it to harmonize with the descending axes of the fruit, ink bottle, and floor line on this side of the picture, in quiet collusion.

    The peerless simplicity of the *Blue Vase* owes much to the strength of its design; and this, in turn, was dependent upon the arrangement of objects Cézanne laid out before him, prior to picking up his palette and brushes. It was often at this stage of the creative procedure that the success or failure of one of his works was determined. This may be seen if one compares the *Blue Vase* with another flower piece of these

92 same years that the artist left unfinished. In the latter the vase of flowers is placed to one side and balanced only by a faintly patterned background at the left – an arrangement which creates an emptiness and imbalance on this side of the picture that even Cézanne's resourceful colourism might never have remedied. From such comparative 'failures' as this, one learns how decisively important to the outcome of a picture was the artist's initial choice of motif.

    If this was true in the intimate art of still life, it was even more so in landscape, with its wider vistas, more complex range of elements, and changing conditions of light and atmosphere. Here Cézanne could not assemble his composition but only *choose* it; and on that choice, too, often depended the success of the picture. Crucial to his choice of motif were not only the 'well balanced' lines he had admired on his outing with Gibert but the potential for formal coherence and integration presented by the entire scene unfolded to his senses. This led Cézanne, in a letter to Zola of May 1883, to distinguish between a 'beautiful view' and a 'motif' when choosing his landscape subjects. Later in life the artist demonstrated what he meant by the latter in conversation with Joachim Gasquet:

> 'You see, a motif is this . . .' (He put his hands together . . . drew them apart, the ten fingers open, then slowly, very slowly brought them together again, clasped them, squeezed them tightly, meshing them.) 'That's what one should try to achieve . . . If one hand is held too high or too low, it won't work. Not a single link should be too slack, leaving a hole through which the emotion, the light, the truth can escape. You must understand that I work on the whole canvas, on everything at once. With one impulse, with undivided faith, I approach all the scattered bits and pieces . . . Everything we see falls apart, vanishes, doesn't it? Nature is always the same, but nothing in her that appears to us, lasts. Our art must render the thrill of her permanence along with her elements, the appearance of all her changes. It must give us a taste of her eternity.'

In the landscapes of the 1880s one observes Cézanne moving increasingly from views of a subject to 'motifs', not least when portraying two of his favourite natural sites, the Gulf of Marseilles seen from l'Estaque and the prominent peak of the Mont Sainte-Victoire.

Characteristic of the artist's early paintings of the Gulf of Marseilles is a preference for broad, open compositions which present a panoramic view of the coast surmounted by sea, distant hills, and a cloudless sky. This 'scenic' approach to the subject, which treats the foreground land mass in a relatively undifferentiated manner, may be seen in a fine version of this theme which still employs the diagonal *94* gradient of strokes typical of the years 1879–82. In a series of slightly later views of the same subject, datable to 1882–85, Cézanne views the coastline and hills through framing trees, which provide a greater *97* focus for the composition and align themselves with the houses and chimneys of the townscape beyond. Often the branches of these trees intertwine along the top of the picture (V. 425, 427), like the clenched

92 *Still Life with a Vase of Flowers,* c. 1885

fingers of Cézanne's own hands in the conversation reported by Gasquet. This traditionally classical means of framing and containing a landscape composition adds to the harmony and finality of these works and paves the way for the even more heroic views of this subject Cézanne was to produce at the end of the 1880s.

Enhancing the grandeur and gravity of many of Cézanne's finest landscapes of this period are the architectural elements he frequently introduces into them, as though to contrast the wayward and irregular forms of the natural world with the more orderly, geometric shapes of man's own devising. The latter dominate a series of views of the hillside town of Gardanne, ten kilometres south of

93 *The Blue Vase, c.* 1885

94 *The Gulf of Marseilles seen from l'Estaque*, 1879–82

Aix, where Cézanne worked in 1885 and 1886, in which the hillside site, surmounted by buildings, appears nestled in the surrounding valley. In two views of Gardanne (V. 431 & 432), Cézanne chose a vertical format dominated by the cubic forms of the buildings, their edges interlocking to create the edifice of the picture in a rhythmic and near-abstract manner. In the most imposing view of all, however, he portrays the town and surrounding countryside from a more distant vantage point. Yet even here the forms of the trees are made to conform to the solid, geometric shapes of the buildings.

The dignity and austerity of Cézanne's art of the mid-1880s also owe much to a change in his technique which may be seen if one compares the *View of Gardanne* with *Le Château de Médan* of five years earlier. In the latter, the rhythmic, parallel brushwork of Cézanne's 'constructive' phase serves to lend an overall surface unity to the picture; but it achieves this only by sacrificing the integrity of

114

95 *View of Gardanne*, 1885–86

96 *View of Gardanne*, 1885–86

97 *L'Estaque*, 1882–85

individual elements to a consistent method of paint application. By the mid-1880s, however, Cézanne had evolved a means of handling which permitted him to describe the character of individual forms in a more flexible and functional manner. Rather than rendering them all in the same basic technique, he allowed the direction of his stroke to follow the contours of a form while still remaining equally visible

98 *The Arc Valley*, 1885–87

99 *Mont Sainte-Victoire*, 1885–87

throughout the picture, thus ensuring its overall unity. With this development the artist could attend both to the formal distinctions between things and the relations among them. The result was a harmony of colour and composition which makes Cézanne's canvases of this period among his most satisfying and deeply considered works.

To none of the artist's creations does this apply more than to his masterly views of the Mont Sainte-Victoire of these years. As with his paintings of l'Estaque these begin, around 1882, with several canvases *100* which portray the mountain merely as part of a more all-embracing scene. By the middle of the decade, however, Cézanne was exploring a number of ways in which it could be made the compositional focus of a picture. In what are probably the earliest of these the mountain's profile is contrasted with a group of foreground trees. This is the *98* arrangement adopted in a thumbnail sketch which shows the Mont Sainte-Victoire off to the left with a solitary pine occupying the centre of the composition. In a remarkably fluid watercolour of this period (RWC 239) Cézanne focuses upon the form of this tree seen against the viaduct and distant hills, whose expansive lines converge upon the tufted contours of the tree. Finally, in a justly celebrated canvas of this *99* theme, the artist daringly bisects the composition with a slanting tree whose crown echoes the shape of the mountain. At the centre right a branch of foliage aligns itself with the road traversing the valley; while, in the middle distance, the viaduct converges with the trunk of the tree, emerging at the left as the 'branch' of a tuft of foliage suspended above the valley. Thus, the three main spatial planes in the landscape appear linked with the foreground pine in a finely calibrated composition of a strength, serenity, and completeness rare even for Cézanne.

The abiding unity of this picture testifies to a deep love of his native countryside that had its origins in Cézanne's youth. 'Do you remember the pine tree which, planted on the bank of the Arc, bowed its shaggy head above the steep slope extending at its feet?', enquired the artist to Zola in April 1858. 'This pine, which protected our bodies with its foliage from the blaze of the sun, ah! may the gods preserve it from the fatal stroke of the woodcutter's axe.'

In his paintings of thirty years later Cézanne's close identification with the landscape of Provence takes on a much more impersonal form. Humanity is banished from the scene and the landscape bathed in an eternal, noon-day light and seen under a cloudless sky. This deprives it of all those accidents of life which might root it in a particular time or place, or under specific conditions of weather. As a

100 *Mont Sainte-Victoire, c.* 1882

result, it is no longer a landscape to inhabit or seek shelter in, but simply one to behold. Nor is it difficult to see how Cézanne creates this impression. Renouncing himself before his subject and abandoning all his preconceptions about nature, he seeks instead to rediscover its intrinsic beauty and significance. At this stage he is able to communicate a love emptied of desire and to portray a truly universal vision of nature.

Two other great canvases (V. 454 & 455) and a preparatory watercolour (RWC 241) of 1885–87 show the heroic profile of the Mont Sainte-Victoire framed to either side by trees whose branches unfurl ecstatically across the sky echoing the contours of the mountain. Like the previous picture, both of these were painted from an elevated viewpoint to the southwest of Aix, presumably from a hill at Bellevue, the estate which Cézanne's brother-in-law Maxime

Conil had purchased in 1881 and where the artist himself often visited and painted during these years.

101   In the most dramatic of these Cézanne sets the mountain firmly in the centre of the composition, its heroic majesty crowning the valley below and seemingly determining the accents and stresses – the weights and balances – of all other elements in the landscape. At the left the trunk of a pine bends as it converges with the contour of the mountain, its descending branches and foliage reaching out towards the orderly roads and fields which traverse the valley. Immediately below these, a solitary house declares itself, linking tree with mountain at a key juncture in the composition. And, sustaining the decorative unity of the picture throughout are the blues, greens, pinks, and ochres which permeate the entire design, rendering the sky as rich and complex in colour as the mountain and valley below.

So inevitable appear all these relations and these interchanges of hue that the picture possesses the harmony and equilibrium of the great classical landscape paintings of Cézanne's seventeenth-century pre-
102   decessors, above all Poussin. Later in life, Cézanne confessed that he wished 'to re-do Poussin over again according to nature' or 'to

101 *Mont Sainte-Victoire*, 1885–87

102 Nicolas Poussin, *Landscape with the Widow of Phocion gathering his Ashes*, 1648

become classical by way of nature, that is to say by sensation'; and herein rested one of the greatest creative challenges of his career. For whereas Poussin's classicism was evolved in the studio, through the joint efforts of the intellect and imagination, Cézanne's had to be won directly from nature. In this respect it was a kind of instinctive – or 'spontaneous' – classicism, one which was *found* rather than *made*.

Moreover, not content simply to imbue his pictures with the grandeur and stability of the classical landscapes of Poussin, Cézanne also sought to infuse them with a sense of the pulsing life of nature – to express (in his own words) both 'the thrill of her permanence' and 'the appearance of all her changes'. In the *Mont Sainte-Victoire* these contrasting faces of nature are apparent in the order and finality of the composition and the vitality of the colour and handling. These endow the landscape with a sense of both permanence and change and combine the concerns of the classical landscape tradition with those of the late nineteenth century. Small wonder that, within a year of Cézanne's death, Maurice Denis would dub him 'the Poussin of Impressionism'.

Created (as we shall see) during the unhappiest years of his maturity, Cézanne's views of the Mont Sainte-Victoire of the mid-1880s reveal the extent to which the artist had at last found refuge in nature – and gained mastery as his reward.

CHAPTER FIVE

Working in Silence (1886–1895)

Cézanne had always sought solace through art. But never before did it afford him a greater escape from the tribulations of life than during 1885–86. How else to explain the fact that such serene and harmonious creations as *The Blue Vase* and the Metropolitan Museum's *Mont Sainte-Victoire* came into being during the greatest personal crisis of his middle years?

93, 99

Early in 1885, Cézanne suffered a severe attack of neuralgia which left him with 'only moments of lucidity'. At about the same time he fell in love with an unidentified woman, to whom he addressed an impassioned letter in spring 1885, confessing himself 'tortured by anxiety'. During the next few months, he enlisted Zola's help in receiving letters from this woman and diverting them to a secret address. Soon after, Cézanne and his family escaped to La Roche-Guyon, where the disturbed artist found it impossible to work. Though nothing is known of the later course of this relationship, it evidently came to nothing; for, by August 1885, Cézanne confessed to Zola: 'for me, there is complete isolation. The brothel in town, or something like that, but nothing more . . .' His appetites appeased in this way, Cézanne once again found himself able to paint and, in the same letter, noted that he was going daily to Gardanne, where (as we have seen) he created some of the most uncompromising landscapes of his career.

Deeply shaken by his unhappy romance, and urged on by his family to legalize his relationship with his mistress, Cézanne and Hortense Fiquet were married at a small civic ceremony on 28 April 1886, the artist's aged father having finally agreed to acknowledge their liaison. Six months later, on 23 October 1886, Louis-Auguste died, aged 88, leaving his son as head of the family and a wealthy man, a position Cézanne himself repeatedly acknowledged, saying: 'My father was a man of genius; he left me with an income of 25,000 francs.'

Cézanne's greatest loss of these years, however, was his friendship with Zola. In spring 1886, the latter published the fourteenth of his series of Rougon-Macquart novels, *L'Oeuvre*, which is centred on the life of the creative artist. Its principal character, Claude Lantier, is a painter, described by Zola in his preliminary notes for the novel as one 'who is never satisfied, who is tormented by his inability to give birth to his own genius, and who in the end kills himself before his unrealized masterpiece. He will not be an impotent artist, but a creator whose ambition is too great, who tries to include all of nature in a single canvas, and who dies in the attempt.'

If Zola's description outlines the broad course of his novel, it conceals the fact that this was to be his most overtly autobiographical work – one in which virtually all the characters are modelled on members of his immediate circle and in which Claude Lantier's boyhood, shared with an aspiring writer named Sandoz, is manifestly indebted to Zola's reminiscences of his early friendship and experiences with Cézanne. Though Claude himself contains character traits of both Manet and Monet, he is most directly modelled on Cézanne and appears to reflect Zola's own belief that his lifelong friend was a creative failure. This is particularly apparent in passages like this, where Sandoz is led to reflect on his changed relationship with Claude over the years:

> At first he had been amazed, for he had had greater faith in his friend than in himself; ever since their schooldays he had considered himself inferior to Claude, whom he looked up to as one of the masters who would revolutionize the art of a whole epoch. Then his heart had been wrung by the spectacle of failing genius, and surprise had given way to bitter compassion for the unspeakable torments of impotence. Was it ever possible, in art, to say where madness lay? he wondered.

Whatever may have been Zola's motivation in writing *L'Oeuvre*, which is anything but a masterpiece of fiction, its tale of the abortive struggles and eventual suicide of an artist dedicated to the realist cause in painting incensed his contemporaries, who saw it as evidence of Zola's disillusionment with the Impressionist group. Monet and Pissarro both denounced it on these grounds; Degas simply regarded it as proof that Zola considered the writers of his day superior to the painters. Cézanne alone – though surely the most wounded of all – remained silent on the matter. All that remains of his remarks on the work is a letter of April 1886, acknowledging receipt of the book:

> I have just received *L'Oeuvre* which you were kind enough to send to me. I thank the author of the 'Rougon-Macquart' for this kind

103 *Self-Portrait,*
c. 1888–90

token of remembrance and ask him to allow me to press his hand in memory of old times. Ever yours under the impulse of years gone by.

Paul Cézanne

Both the formality and the elegiac tone of this letter, which nowhere alludes to the content of Zola's novel, signal a new note in Cézanne's relationship with the writer. Prey to the most profound misgivings about his own creative efforts, and having regularly confided these to his long-time friend, Cézanne may well have regarded the appearance of *L'Oeuvre* as an act of betrayal. So far as we know, no further communication ever passed between them; and, as late as 1896, Zola described Cézanne in print as an 'abortive great painter'. Yet when the novelist died in a tragic accident in September 1902 Cézanne shut himself in his studio all day, weeping.

If the publication of *L'Oeuvre* precipitated the final rupture between Cézanne and Zola, signs of a growing divide between them had been evident for years; for the awkward and insecure Cézanne can have felt himself no match for the worldly, affluent, and highly successful Zola. An even greater divide was their aesthetic outlook. Whereas Zola had always stressed the importance of 'ideas' in painting and shown little understanding of the aesthetic values of his friend's canvases, Cézanne grew increasingly suspicious of what he called the 'literary spirit' in painting – one which, he noted in later life, 'so often causes the painter to deviate from his true path – the concrete study of nature – to lose himself in intangible speculation.'

One further connection between Cézanne and Zola's novel needs emphasizing – and this was perhaps the most painful of all. The plot of *L'Oeuvre* is clearly modelled on Balzac's short story, *Le chef-d'oeuvre inconnu* of 1831, which recounts the tale of the mad genius Frenhofer, who has laboured all his life on a single painting and, in the process, destroys it by reducing it to an incoherent mass of lines and colours representing nothing. Like Claude Lantier – and like Cézanne himself – Balzac's hero pursues an inner vision of beauty and artistic perfection which ultimately seems always to elude him and leads Frenhofer, too, to commit suicide. Cézanne was certainly familiar with Balzac's short story. Not only did he confess himself most drawn to Frenhofer among all fictional characters but he paraphrased many of the latter's statements on art in his own letters. Moreover, later in life the mere mention of Frenhofer's name was sufficient to reduce the aged master to tears. Given his close identification with Balzac's abortive genius, Cézanne may well have regarded Zola's reincarnation of this figure in Claude Lantier as final confirmation that his own creative efforts were likewise regarded as doomed by his contemporaries and that his fear of following in Frenhofer's footsteps had been tragically well founded.

Cézanne's disturbed state of mind in the months immediately following the appearance of Zola's novel is evident from a letter to Chocquet of May 1886. 'I should have wished to possess the intellectual equilibrium that characterizes you and allows you to achieve with certainty the desired end,' confesses the artist in a mood of self-defeat, '. . . I am struck by this serenity . . . Fate has not endowed me with an equal stability, that is the only regret I have about the things of this earth.'

Fate had, however, endowed Cézanne with a total commitment to his art. This was to prove his only defence against the warring elements of his own temperament and of the world at large. It is revealed to us in the most formidably austere of all the artist's self-portraits – and the only one to show him with attributes of his profession – datable to exactly these years. In this Cézanne portrays himself shielded behind his palette and easel, the contour of the former continuing the line of his arm as an extension of his very being. Staring out at us with a mask-like expression of almost inhuman fixity, the constraining lines of Cézanne's head and body appear welded to the rectangles which surround him. Barricaded in a world of art, Cézanne here displays those qualities of control, self-denial, and tremendous inner strength which (*pace* his letter to Chocquet) made it possible for him too 'to achieve with certainty the desired end'.

103

In the same letter the artist confesses that his 'end' remained the same. 'As for the rest', observes Cézanne, 'I have nothing to complain about. Always the sky, the boundless things of nature, attract me and give me the chance to look with pleasure . . . To conclude, I must tell you that I am still occupied with my painting and that there are treasures to be taken away from this country, which has not yet found an interpreter equal to the abundance of riches which it displays.'

Increasingly disillusioned with the world of Paris, Cézanne spent the better part of the late 1880s in Aix, where, after his father's death, he was forced to tend his aged mother. From these years date a large number of views of the Jas de Bouffan and its immediate surroundings, with the artist continuing to show a fondness for the avenue of chestnut trees lining the back of the family estate, which afforded him such a rhythmically ordered subject. He also returned to l'Estaque to paint his grandest views of the town and surrounding bay, ringed on the horizon by distant hills. Like his views of Gardanne of 1885–86, these reveal a striking preoccupation with the most architectonic features of the landscape.

104

In one, the cubic forms of a group of buildings frame the scene below, forming a stable base for the composition. The central one of these is the most solidly modelled form in the entire picture and, in the lines of its roof, introduces a series of diagonals which link the foreground townscape to the mountains beyond. Further linking all elements of the scene are the subtly nuanced changes of colour, which lead the shoreline at the left to grow bluer as it approaches the sea and the tall smokestack immediately below it likewise to mediate between the warm hues of the buildings and the prevailing blues and greys of the upper portions of the picture. But the most unexpected elements of all are the cast shadow of the chimney on the central building and

104 *The Gulf of Marseilles seen from l'Estaque, c.* 1888

the puff of smoke at the right – both of them fugitive effects normally excluded from Cézanne's timeless vision. Here, however, they are aligned with the form of a distant jetty, creating an invisible diagonal which connects foreground with distance to strengthen the overall harmony of the composition. Peace and serenity pervade this heroic landscape and suggest that it was Cézanne's culminating view of l'Estaque; for, after the 1880s, the artist chose never to work at this site, where he deplored the effects of modern industrialization.

In 1888, Cézanne paid a visit to Paris and the surrounding countryside. There he painted several views of the banks of the Marne (V. 629–32) and of a tree-lined avenue at Chantilly (V. 626–28) – the northern equivalent of the avenue at the Jas de Bouffan. In the following year Renoir and his family visited Cézanne at Aix and the two painted together outdoors. Since Renoir was renting the estate of

105 (left above) Auguste Renoir, *Mont Sainte-Victoire*, 1889

106 (left) *Mont Sainte-Victoire*, 1888–90

107 (above) *Provençal Landscape*, 1885–87

108 (right) *Mont Sainte-Victoire seen from the Wall of the Jas de Bouffan*, 1885–88

127, 128 Cézanne's brother-in-law at Bellevue, they were inevitably drawn to views of this site, with its picturesque pigeon tower and windswept pines. But they also painted a number of views of the Mont Sainte-Victoire which, when compared, reveal how far Cézanne had grown from his former fellow Impressionists.

105 In Renoir's canvases of this theme, the artist revels in the tropical beauty of the spot, in one instance (Barnes Foundation, Merion, Pa.) portraying peasants working and resting in the fields at the base of the mountain, and, in another, tingeing the tips of the trees and mountain with golden sunlight and rendering the whole with a feathery lightness of touch which captures the most evanescent features of the scene.

106 In Cézanne's mighty views of this same theme, however, the mountain is endowed with an impregnable authority. Seen now from an unimpeded viewpoint across the valley of the Arc, the Mont Sainte-Victoire transcends considerations of time or place and appears elevated to a more universal plane. Moreover, minus the framing trees and encircling branches of his paintings on this theme of 1885–87, Cézanne explores a subtler way of relating the foreground trees

109 (far left) *Portrait of Madame Cézanne*, 1887–90

110 (left) *Madame Cézanne in a Conservatory*, 1887–90

111 *Portrait of Madame Cézanne*, c. 1890

and buildings to the prominent façade of the mountain. As in his great view of the Gulf of Marseilles, he relies upon a series of formal and colouristic connections to link all elements of the scene, the coiling contours of the trees echoing those of the mountain to give the landscape an unparalleled majesty.

To be sure, not all of Cézanne's landscapes of this (or any other) period of his career are as successfully integrated as these; for here – as in his choice of still-life subjects – the artist remained dependent upon his choice of motif. Another Provençal landscape of these years *107* demonstrates the difficulties Cézanne faced when confronted with a less coherent scene. Though studiously framed by groups of trees, the landscape recedes to a low-lying expanse of fields and hills that affords scant opportunity for the structural integration of many of his finest pictures. When the artist applies this same basic compositional scheme to a view of the Mont Sainte-Victoire, however, the contour of the *108* mountain fits snugly into the overhanging branches of the trees, which it almost resembles, and provides a crucial focus for the composition.

The cessation of Cézanne's correspondence with Zola leaves many gaps in our knowledge of the artist's personal life and whereabouts during the late 1880s. We do know that Cézanne's mother remained on bad terms with Hortense Fiquet, who often chose to live apart from her husband during these years. When the family was together, however, Cézanne rarely lost an opportunity to portray his wife and son, now nearing the end of his teens. In fact, Madame Cézanne remains the artist's favourite sitter of these years, her patience and forbearance seemingly unwavering in posing motionlessly for her husband. In drawings of her, Cézanne continues to explore a wide range of poses and moods, some of which reveal a careworn, if soulful figure of ineffable sadness. The more formal and prolonged sittings required for his paintings, however, generally elicited a more detached response from the artist. In the most characteristic of these, Madame Cézanne is seated erect, her hands in her lap, with her oval face, expressionless features and severely parted hair rendering her both inert and impassive. In a succession of works in this vein spanning the late 1880s and early 1890s, Cézanne's view of the sitter scarcely alters, though he frequently changes the background against which she is seen. As much as anything, this alters the nature of the characterization. Viewed against a setting of foliage and flowers, she assumes a tender and submissive air, almost wistful in its mood of fading youth and beauty. When seen against a plainer background, however, Madame Cézanne appears remote and inscrutable, her stylized features and unfocused gaze resembling those of a Buddhist sage.

Perhaps in response to the sitter's more unpredictable nature, Cézanne's portraits of his son of this period appear somewhat more varied in mood and inventive in pose. One of them shows young Paul posed proudly and seen in full-length, as though modelling a new suit of clothes. The assertive stance of this drawing recurs in one of the artist's most unexpected creations of these years, *Mardi Gras* of 1888, which portrays his son (at the right) as Harlequin and the family friend, Louis Guillaume, as Pierrot. Though Cézanne had evinced some interest in the world of the *commedia dell'arte* at the start of his career, the choice of this theme in the late 1880s may have been inspired by his son's own fondness for donning fancy dress and engaging in amateur theatricals in his playful teens. A series of drawings (Ch. 935–37), executed in a hurly-burly manner befitting the high-spirited antics of the Italian comedy, also dates from this period. When Cézanne came to create the ambitious and uncharacteristic canvas of 1888, however, he proceeded more methodically, making a magnificent sequence of studies in pencil, watercolour and

109
110
111
112
113
114

132

oil in preparation for the final painting (Ch. 938–41; RWC 295; V. 553–55). Though the latter is breathtaking in colour, it is pervaded by a curiously joyless mood which seems at odds with the theme. Yet it is consistent with an approach to figure painting that Cézanne was increasingly to explore during the final phase of his career.

This is already apparent in a series of paintings and watercolours the artist made of an Italian peasant boy during the same period. All of these show the figure dressed in a bright red waistcoat and posed pensively before a richly coloured background. In two watercolours of this sitter (RWC 375 & 376) Cézanne portrays him seated frontally against a green background, the complementary contrast of red and green adding a liveliness to the work that is in marked contrast to the sitter's languid mood. This approach appears accentuated in four paintings of the same youth (V. 680–83), one of which shows him seated, head in hand, in a traditionally melancholy pose. Wearing a *119* red and yellow waistcoat and blue breeches, the figure appears against a setting of greens, whites, and blues – the brilliance of the colour providing an obvious foil for the sitter's introspective mood. This daring combination of inner life and outer display is reminiscent of the devices employed by Rembrandt in many of his greatest portraits, where a similar principle of 'intensification by contrast' adds to the emotional range and depth of the characterization. As such, Cézanne's studies of this Italian peasant boy are among the first works of his maturity to explore the pictorial strategies and more subjective states of mind of his later portraits.

There is little in the elegiac mood of these pictures to indicate that Cézanne's own artistic fortunes had undergone a perceptible shift during these years. Yet this is exactly what happened in Paris in 1888. In that year, the critic J. K. Huysmans published an article containing a favourable mention of the artist. Though Huysmans had described Cézanne as 'one of the Impressionists who didn't make the grade' as recently as 1883 – doubtless reflecting in this the views of his friend Zola – he now spoke of the artist as a 'too much ignored painter'. The next year Huysmans devoted a whole chapter to Cézanne in his book *Certains*, describing him as 'a revealing colourist who contributed more than the late Manet to the Impressionist movement'. In 1889 a picture by Cézanne was also exhibited at the Paris World's Fair; and, in the same year, the artist was invited to participate in an exhibition of the young Belgian group, Les XX, in Brussels, along with Sisley and Van Gogh. Though flattered by this invitation, Cézanne's letter of acceptance to the exhibition's organizer, Octave Maus, is

112 *Full-length Portrait of the*
Artist's Son, c. 1885

characteristically tetchy and defensive in its explanation of his reluctance to show his works. 'As the many studies to which I have dedicated myself have given me only negative results', pleads the artist, 'and as I am afraid of only too justified criticism, I had resolved to work in silence until the day when I should feel myself able to defend theoretically the result of my attempts.'

Three pictures by Cézanne were exhibited in Brussels in 1890, where they drew little notice, leaving the artist with just a few more years to continue 'to work in silence'. Outwardly, however, these were among the most eventful years of his career. In the summer of 1890, Cézanne made his only trip abroad, spending five months in Switzerland with his wife and son. At about this time he began to suffer from diabetes, which was increasingly to plague him in later life. Under the influence of his sister Marie, he also became a devout Catholic, regularly attending mass. During the early 1890s he divided his time between Paris and Aix, where he lived apart from his wife and son, preferring instead to inhabit the Jas de Bouffan with his

113 *Mardi Gras*, 1888

114 Studies for *Mardi Gras*, c. 1888

mother and elder sister. Visited there by his boyhood friend Numa Coste in 1891, he was described by the latter as 'timid, primitive and younger than ever . . . it is one of the most touching things I have ever experienced, to see how this brave boy has preserved his childlike naiveté, forgetting his disappointments in the struggle for life – in resignation and suffering – stubbornly pursuing the work which he does not succeed in bringing off.'

A more graphic account of Cézanne's vulnerable and unworldly nature emerges in a description of the artist by the American painter, Mary Cassatt, who met him at an inn in Giverny in 1894:

> . . . when I first saw him I thought he looked like a cut-throat with large red eyeballs standing out from his head in a most ferocious manner, a rather fierce-looking pointed beard, quite gray, and an

115 *Five Female Bathers*, 1885–87

116 *Male Bathers*, 1890–94

excited way of talking that positively made the dishes rattle. I found later on that I had misjudged his appearance, for far from being fierce or a cut-throat, he has the gentlest nature possible, 'comme un enfant' as he would say. His manners at first rather startled me – he scrapes his soup plate, then lifts it and pours the remaining drops in the spoon; he even takes his chop in his fingers and pulls the meat from the bone. He eats with his knife and accompanies every gesture, every movement of his hand, with that implement, which he grasps firmly when he commences his meal and never puts down until he leaves the table. Yet in spite of the total disregard of the dictionary of manners, he shows a politeness towards us which no other man here would have shown. He will not allow Louise to serve him before us in the usual order of succession at the table; he is even deferential to that stupid maid, and he pulls off the old tam-o'-shanter, which he wears to protect his bald head, when he enters the room.

117 *A Card Player*, 1890–92

118 (opposite) *The Card Players*, 1890–92

Cézanne's deference to ordinary humanity is also apparent in his art of this period, which increasingly shows a preference for depicting local peasants and workmen, this being the only sector of society with which the humble and reclusive artist apparently felt at ease. Around 1890 Cézanne embarked upon a series of card-player compositions, which were to occupy him until about 1894, showing from two to five figures grouped around a table engaged in this familiar pastime. Though the subject was a favourite one in seventeenth-century art – not least with the Le Nain brothers, whose works Cézanne is certain to have known – earlier masters had invariably portrayed it as a theme of trickery and deceit and stressed its anecdotal and moralizing elements. Cézanne, on the other hand, makes of it one of the most solemn and meditative themes of his career and, as he progresses through the series, eliminates all traces of narrative to concentrate upon essentials.

The first of these (V. 560) is the largest multi-figure picture the

138

artist had ever undertaken and shows three men seated around a table
watched over by a standing peasant and a young boy, the different
ages of the onlookers retaining a vestige of the seventeenth-century
tradition of treating this theme, where youthful curiosity was often
contrasted with mature omniscience. In a second version, less than
half the size, Cézanne reduces the composition to four figures,
eliminating the boy, and focuses more closely upon the central action.
For both of these pictures – as for the two-figure versions of the theme
– the artist made a number of studies in pencil, watercolour and oil
remarkable for their self-absorbed poses and utter stillness.

These same qualities inform Cézanne's three final versions of this
theme (V. 556–58), which are confined to two figures seated to either
side of a table whose central axis is marked by a solitary bottle.
Though the sequence of these works is uncertain and their sizes vary,
there is general consensus that they progress towards the version in the
Musée d'Orsay, the smallest and most concentrated of all. In this the

118

117, 122

121

119 *Boy with a Red Waistcoat,*
1889–90

120 *Kitchen Still Life,* 1888–90

121 *The Card Players*, 1892–94

122 *Man with a Pipe*, 1892–94

symmetrical arrangement of all these compositions is subtly shifted by the tilt of the tabletop and bottle and the cropping of the figure at the right to create a more dynamically balanced arrangement similar to certain of Cézanne's still lifes of these years. The colour too is of an indescribable subtlety. Whereas Cézanne had employed the full range of his palette in the four- and five-figure versions of this theme, those with only two card-players are confined to a near-monochromatic range of hues – purples, deep browns and reds, blacks and ochres – of a seemingly infinite delicacy. Transcending all the conventions of 'genre' painting from which they ultimately derive, Cézanne's card-player pictures possess a contemplative seriousness which calls to mind the noblest themes of the past and led the great English critic Roger Fry to describe them as containing 'the gravity, the reserve and the weighty solemnity of some monument of antiquity.' Fry was also aware that it was the very starkness and ineloquence of these pictures that endowed them with their epic stature and recalled the most monumental masters of the past. 'The simplicity of the disposition', he observed of the Musée d'Orsay picture, in a particularly memorable comparison, 'is such as might even have made Giotto hesitate to adopt it.'

The grandeur and economy of Cézanne's card-player compositions also mark his bather pictures of the middle years. Though relatively few in number these reveal the artist developing his ideas for this theme towards an ever-increasing monumentality, as though seeking a definitive solution to a compositional problem that had haunted him for nearly two decades. In his most important canvas of 115 female bathers of this period, datable to 1885–87, Cézanne adapts the pyramidal figure groups of the late 1870s to a design of almost terrifying austerity, in which five ungainly nudes fill the scene in tightly interlocking poses and landscape is almost entirely eliminated. Carefully prepared from a squared compositional drawing (Ch. 517) and set within a canvas which is itself exactly square, the arrangement of the figures in this picture possesses a confrontational quality that seems to lay bare all the artist's deepest fears about the threatening power of women. In its brutal simplification of the human form and its near-menacing eroticism, the canvas most obviously recalls the 23 equally repellent nudes in Cézanne's early *Temptation of St Anthony*.

Much less emotionally charged are a group of compositions of male bathers of the early 1890s which show the familiar frieze-like arrangement Cézanne favoured for these pictures, the figures wading, standing, or seated in rhythmically alternating poses. The largest and

123 *Still Life with a Basket of Apples*, 1890–94

most fully resolved of these portrays the figures against a background   *116*
of clouds and trees which serves further to articulate their poses and
actions and differs from the enclosed, woodland settings of the early
groups of male bathers. In addition to adding to the clarity and
spaciousness of the effect, this more open and differentiated setting
anticipates the backgrounds of Cézanne's final bather pictures, where
landscape and the human figure enjoy equal prominence.

   If the bather pictures of this period build upon the solutions of the
past, Cézanne's still lifes of *c.* 1890 appear much more innovative and
experimental. This is already apparent in the *Kitchen Still Life* of 1888–   *120*
90, which includes a larger and more complex assemblage of objects
than any earlier still life by the artist and introduces another new
development of these years. Heretofore, Cézanne's still-life compositions had always been arranged parallel to the picture plane, with the

143

124 *The Great Pine,* 1892–96

background wall serving to seal off the space and concentrate attention on the objects set before it. In the *Kitchen Still Life,* however, Cézanne sets these in a deep space which recedes diagonally into the picture and itself contains objects which may be related to those of the central still life, thereby stressing both the artifice of the construction and the harmony of the overall surface design. At the top and sides of the picture the legs of a chair and two tables converge upon the fruit and vessels in the foreground, as though to refute the illusionism of the scene. And, at the upper left a portion of a decorative screen depicting fruit and flowers echoes the rounded forms of the fruit on the table

144

and establishes a subsidiary diagonal from upper left to lower right which counterbalances the more assertive diagonal running along the opposite axis of the picture. Most wonderful of all are the round, rhyming shapes which the artist's sensuous intelligence uncovers throughout the scene. These link the fruit, vessels, and drapery in a constantly evolving harmony which, as so often in Cézanne's art, seems to pose yet further possibilities. Scarcely less resourceful is the formal play on the curved and crisscrossing rhythms of the wickerwork of the basket and ginger pot. In one instance 'confused' with the stem of a pear and (at the upper left) inverted in the descending loop of a band of ribbon, these function as a sub-theme in the composition, combining the rounded contours of the organic forms with the colours and axes of the man-made objects which surround them.

Cézanne's growing preference for a more dynamic and elaborate grouping of still-life objects takes a somewhat different form in the magnificent *Still Life with a Basket of Apples* of 1890–94, which, like *123* the *Kitchen Still Life*, deservedly bears the artist's signature. Though this work reverts to the planar and symmetrical arrangement of elements characteristic of the mid-1880s, its dramatically tilting bottle and descending tabletop add a potential imbalance to the construction which is counterpoised by the steeply rising basket and the carefully aligned biscuits at the right. The latter in turn appear joined to the central axis of the picture by a darkened passage of shadow which links them with the bulging contour of the bottle. Though the distortions introduced into such pictures as this have been attributed to everything from the artist's shifting viewpoint while working to his defective eyesight, a more convincing explanation was offered by Meyer Schapiro, who observed of them: 'Such deviations make the final equilibrium of the picture seem more evidently an achievement of the artist rather than an imitation of an already existing stability in nature.'

An even more searching exploration of the relationship between nature and artifice is the *Still Life with a Plaster Cupid* of 1892–95. Here *125* Cézanne assembles familiar still-life objects – apples and onions – around the base of a plaster statuette in his possession. Formerly attributed to Pierre Puget, this is more likely to be by François Duquesnoy and was often drawn and painted by the artist during *126* these years. Surrounding the central still life is a series of canvases. At the rear appears a painted copy of another plaster cast Cézanne owned – that of a flayed man, attributed to Michelangelo and also often *143*

126 (above) *Plaster Cupid, c.* 1890

125 *Still Life with a Plaster Cupid,* 1892–95

copied by the artist. And, at the extreme left, may be seen a portion of Cézanne's *Still Life with a Peppermint Bottle* of *c.* 1890 (V. 625), one of the artist's most harmonious works of these years.

The combination of a 'real' statuette and a painted copy of one, a 'real' still life and a painted one, introduces a series of paradoxes and ambiguities which Cézanne ultimately resolves within the formal devices of the picture by obliterating all such distinctions and considering the objects simply as a 'motif' – though not without irony. Thus, the main lines of the painted still life converge upon the plaster cupid, the onion at the left elides with the table leg in the painting while still being cut by the diagonal canvas edge, and the fictive drapery of the painted still life spills out on to the table, linking 'illusion' with 'reality' within the overall artifice of the painting. Similarly the painted copy of the statuette at the rear is related to the 'real' cupid through a prominent green apple, undiminished in size from those in the foreground, whose bulging form and indentation

146

find their equivalent in the cupid's protruding belly and navel. From this endless series of paradoxes and playful allusions (the right foot of the cupid even casting a green, onion-stem-like shadow!) the artist achieves a daring equilibrium between different levels of reality by reducing all of the objects before him to the status of pictorial elements. No less ingenious is the spatial setting in which these objects are seen. Bounded by the tabletop and curving draperies at the left, which echo the base and legs of the plaster cupid, it twists upwards and outwards at the right, as though in response to the spiralling pose and form of the upper portions of this figure.

The early 1890s also mark a transitional phase in Cézanne's development as a landscape painter. Some of his works of these years retain the emotional restraint and monumental clarity of his landscapes of the immediately preceding years. Others veer towards much more subjective moods. Among the former is the *Bellevue Pigeon Tower* of *c.* 1890 (a slightly smaller version of this subject is V. *127* 653). With its clearly bounded forms and compact distribution of masses, this picture is as close as Cézanne ever came to imbuing a landscape subject with the purity and finality of one of his still-life compositions. Rigidly banded into three nearly equal areas of earth, building and sky, the design appears further regimented by the tiered and scalloped shape of the pigeon tower, the contours of which are mirrored in the forms of the surrounding trees. As a comparison with a photograph of the motif makes clear, Cézanne has achieved this *128* effect of Spartan simplicity only by stripping away everything inessential from the scene and allowing abstract considerations completely to override the vagaries of nature. As D.H. Lawrence observed in 1929: 'Sometimes Cézanne builds up a landscape essentially out of omissions.'

The ruthless simplification of form evident in the *Bellevue Pigeon Tower* calls to mind the advice Cézanne gave to the young painter Emile Bernard in 1904: 'treat nature by means of the cylinder, the sphere, the cone, everything brought into proper perspective so that each side of an object or a plane is directed towards a central point.' Though this oft-quoted statement has been seen as anticipating the advent of Cubism and abstract art, it is best understood as a prescription for reducing the imperfect forms of the natural world to essential shapes. Far from being a revolutionary idea, this was a standard method of creating order and harmony in painting. Long sanctioned by tradition and training, it was a method also advocated and practised by Poussin.

127 *The Bellevue Pigeon Tower, c.* 1890

128 Photograph of the Bellevue Pigeon Tower

129 *House with Cracked Walls*, 1892–94

Other landscapes of the early 1890s appear more romantic in mood and theme and anticipate the greater emotionalism of the artist's final years. In the *House with Cracked Walls*, for instance, Cézanne depicts an abandoned house set in a remote, rocky landscape. Deep cracks in the wall of this building resemble the trunks of the surrounding trees, a similarity which may well have struck the artist as reminiscent of the processes of growth and decay in nature. And, in one of the most stirring and impassioned of his landscapes of these years, Cézanne focuses upon a solitary pine in the grounds of his brother-in-law's estate, whose twisted branches indicate that it is a victim of the mistral, the fierce wind which sweeps through Provence from the north, often for days at a time. Defiantly silhouetted against the sky, this tree appears to symbolize the most indomitable forces in nature and, in its heroism and turbulence, reminds us of Cézanne's own fortitude and despair. Further evidence of the artist's empathy with this subject is the fact that he added two strips to the top of the canvas as he went along, as though unable to contain his emotional identification with the theme.

The Great Pine was among the pictures by Cézanne included in Vollard's one-man exhibition of the artist's works in 1895 – an event which marked a turning-point in Cézanne's critical reputation, even if it did little to alter the outer course of his existence. To understand how this event came about, it is necessary to consider the artist's growing reputation during the immediately preceding years.

Despite the fact that the aging Cézanne lived the life of a recluse – with one critic of the time doubting whether he even existed – his works began to attract increased attention among artists and critics during the early 1890s. In 1892, Emile Bernard, a disciple of Gauguin who was soon to become one of Cézanne's greatest admirers, published a short biographical study on the artist. One year later, the critic Gustave Geffroy wrote sympathetically of him in a study of Impressionism and, soon after, observed of the artist:

> For a long time, Cézanne has had a curious artistic fate. He might be described as a person at once unknown and famous, having only rare contact with the public yet considered influential by the restless and the seekers in the field of painting; known only by a few, living in savage isolation, reappearing, then disappearing suddenly from the sight of his intimate friends. All the little-known facts about his life, his almost secret productivity, the rare canvases, which seem to follow none of the accepted rules of publicity, all these give him a

kind of strange renown, already distant; a mystery surrounds his person and his work. Those who are in search of the unfamiliar, who like to discover things that have not yet been seen, speak of Cézanne's canvases with a knowing air, giving information like a password . . . What did his canvases look like? Where could some of them be seen? Reply was made that the preceding week a canvas had been seen at Tanguy's, the dealer in the rue Clauzel, but that it was necessary to hurry to find it for there were always collectors quick to pounce upon these prizes, which were few and far between.

Geffroy was correct in stating that it was only in the shop of the enterprising colour merchant Tanguy that Cézanne's rare canvases could be seen in Paris. There, however, they had been admired and, on occasion, even purchased by many of the new generation of painters, including Van Gogh and Gauguin, Seurat and Signac, Bernard and Maurice Denis.

Tanguy died in 1893. At the sale of his collection, which took place the following spring, six canvases by Cézanne were bought by the then unknown picture dealer, Ambroise Vollard. During the same months, Geffroy published a long and favourable article on the artist, which Cézanne gratefully acknowledged. The moment seemed appropriate, then, for an exhibition of the artist's works in Paris – a task which Vollard willingly undertook.

After experiencing some difficulty in even locating Cézanne, Vollard eventually secured the artist's agreement to send 150 works to an exhibition which opened at the dealer's premises on the rue Lafitte in November 1895. The critical reception to this was decidedly mixed and much of it is recounted in Vollard's biography of the artist, though this lays undue stress upon the more bizarre reactions to Cézanne's work – the first purchaser at the sale, who turned out to have been blind from birth, or the man who forced his wife to look at one of Cézanne's canvases as punishment for a domestic squabble. A letter from Pissarro to his son makes clear, however, that his fellow artists – Renoir, Degas, and Monet – were uniformly enthusiastic about Cézanne's pictures, at last being given belated recognition in the French capital. But perhaps the most poignant vindication of Cézanne's lifelong creative struggles came in an article by the novelist and critic Arsène Alexandre, which bore the revealing title 'Claude Lantier', and observed:

Today it has suddenly been discovered that Zola's friend, the mysterious man from Provence, the painter simultaneously incomplete and inventive, sly and uncivilized, is a great man.

Great man? Not altogether, if one remains aloof from the enthusiasms of the season, but one of the strangest temperaments, from whom a great deal in the new school has been borrowed, knowingly or not. The interesting thing about this exhibition is the influence he exerted on artists who are now well known: Pissarro, Guillaumin, and later, Gauguin, Van Gogh, and others.

From Vollard's exhibition onwards, Cézanne's art was never to be out of favour – or view – of the most advanced painters and critics in Paris. But the artist himself appears initially to have been unaffected by this sudden change in fortune. He was not to be seen at Vollard's first exhibition; and, when he did attend one, four years later, his only recorded remark was: 'It's amazing! He has framed them all.'

Early in 1895, however, Cézanne agreed to paint the portrait of Gustave Geffroy, whose pioneering articles had done so much to bring about this re-evaluation of his achievement. Seated in the very study in which those articles had been written, Geffroy appears absorbed in thought, his pen poised before an open book. Rare among Cézanne's portraits in its emphasis upon the occupational status of the sitter, the portrait was eventually abandoned by the artist, who wrote to Geffroy in June 1895:

> As I am about to depart and cannot bring to a satisfactory conclusion the work which surpasses my strength and which I was wrong to undertake, I would like to ask you to excuse me and to hand over to the messenger whom I shall send to you, the things which I have left in your library.

An even more painful reminder of the degree to which Cézanne's growing reputation had done nothing to ease his creative difficulties – or even to convince him that he was right to have become a painter – is a letter to Monet, written three weeks later:

> I was forced to abandon for the time being the study that I had started at the house of Geffroy, who had placed himself so generously at my disposal, and I am a little upset at the meagre result I obtained, especially after so many sittings and successive bursts of enthusiasm and despair. So here I am then, landed again in the South, from which I should, perhaps, never have separated in order to fling myself into the chimerical pursuit of art.

130 *Portrait of Gustave Geffroy*, 1895

131 *Portrait of Ambroise Vollard*, 1899

CHAPTER SIX

Cézanne and the Old Masters

Four years after abandoning his portrait of Geffroy, Cézanne was commissioned to paint the portrait of the man who had done most to put his art before the public during these years, Ambroise Vollard. *131* This was painted in the artist's studio in Paris and, like that of Geffroy, portrays the sitter as a man of learning and introspection. After 115 sittings during which Vollard was exhorted to sit absolutely still – 'like an apple' – Cézanne abandoned this picture too, leaving two spots of bare canvas on Vollard's right hand. 'If the copy I'm making in the Louvre turns out well', he explained to Vollard, 'perhaps I will be able tomorrow to find the exact tone to cover up those spots. Don't you see, Monsieur Vollard, that if I put something there by guesswork, I might have to paint the whole canvas over starting from that point?' 'The prospect made me tremble', notes Vollard exasperatedly in his biography of the artist; and the two spots remain.

Cézanne's insistence that only his studies in the Louvre could help him through the creative difficulties he encountered when working from nature is a recurring one throughout his career and makes him unique among painters. Of his greatest predecessors only Rubens – Cézanne's favourite painter – served so long an apprenticeship copying the artists of the past; and even the Flemish master abandoned this practice in the later years of his career. In contrast, Cézanne's rate of production in this field actually increases as he grows older. Thus, of the nearly four hundred copies after other artists which survive by him, approximately one-third date from after 1890 – a time when one might have expected him to have exhausted all that tradition could teach. In addition to reminding us of the extent to which he saw his own achievements as building upon those of the past, Cézanne's copies after the Old Masters testify to the constantly questing nature of his creative personality. Few insights into the master are more moving or instructive than the mixture of humility and awe with which he repeatedly consulted the great artists of the past in search of solutions to his own creative dilemmas.

The majority of Cézanne's copies are drawings done in sketch-books during his visits to the Louvre or from the numerous books and

132 *The Dead Christ* (after Fra Bartolommeo), 1866–69

133 *Reclining Male Nude, c.* 1865

reproductions he kept in his studio. As such, they afford the most personal insight into his creative thinking. For drawing – especially in a sketchbook – remained Cézanne's most intimate form of expression. Not only was it small and portable but it permitted him to work rapidly and without concern for the weightier considerations of colour that inevitably affected his oils and watercolours. Indeed, so privately did Cézanne regard his sketchbooks that he often used them over long periods (making it difficult for scholars to date them) and frequently employed them for other purposes, such as doing his accounts, listing the pigments he needed to buy, or even allowing his young son to doodle.

Though Cézanne's copies served many purposes, the most obvious of them was to provide him with a repertoire of ideas for his own imaginary compositions, especially his bather paintings. Given that these often presented him with the greatest problem of invention – and that he was not gifted with the remarkable powers of visualization of the artists he most admired – Cézanne often sought recourse to tradition to enrich the formal vocabulary of his art. Thus, a number of poses recurringly found in his own figure paintings were borrowed from artists as diverse as Signorelli and Delacroix. Occasionally, having alighted upon one of these, Cézanne would then study the same pose from life and stamp it with the force of his own personality. An instance of this is his early *Preparation for a Funeral*, which was inspired by a drawing of the Dead Christ by Fra Bartolommeo that Cézanne copied in the Louvre. At the same time, the artist drew a live model in a similar pose, eventually adopted for the painting. This lacks the grace and rhetoric of the Renaissance prototype and no longer recalls a Christian lamentation but simply the rigor mortis of death. Similarly, around 1880 Cézanne made a painted copy after Delacroix's *Woman at her Toilet* (V. 254), whose pose recurs in any number of his paintings of male and female bathers. In the 1890s, however, he studied the same pose from a live model (V. 710 & RWC 387), as though to check the flights of Delacroix's imagination against the stubborn facts of reality. Rare though such instances are throughout Cézanne's career, they afford literal proof of his own assertion that 'the Louvre is a good book to consult but it must be only an intermediary. The real and immense study to be undertaken is the manifold picture of nature.'

Such direct 'borrowings' aside, Cézanne's study of the Old Masters was motivated by much subtler and more complex considerations, apparent in the changing pattern it assumes at varying stages of his

22

132
133

134 Peter Paul Rubens, *The Apotheosis of Henry IV*, 1622–25

135 *Preparation for a Banquet, c.* 1890

136 Detail from *The
Apotheosis of Henry IV*
(after Rubens), 1864–65

137 *Apotheosis of Delacroix*,
c. 1873

career. This may be summarized as follows. In his student days, seemingly overwhelmed by the many masters and traditions that had preceded him, Cézanne made copies after a wide variety of artists, as though uncertain of where his allegiances lay. As his career progressed, however, the list of artists – and even images – dwindles until a handful of key works occupy his attentions in an almost obsessional manner, apparently containing the clues to the problems he himself faced when struggling to complete his portrait of Vollard.

Doubtless due to the obscurity of the sources available to him during his student days in Aix, few of Cézanne's copies of these years may be readily identified. With his move to Paris in the 1860s, where he immediately began to copy in the Louvre, Cézanne made a number of drawings after major masterpieces – some of which were to haunt him until the end of his career. Thus, among isolated studies after Raphael and Velázquez, neither of whom was to prove an abiding interest, there are already copies after the French seventeenth-century sculptor, Pierre Puget, whom Cézanne was to return to more than any earlier master. Similarly, the painter – and, indeed, the picture – to which he was to devote the largest number of copies is already announced in these years. This is Rubens's *Apotheosis of Henry IV*, one of twenty-one canvases depicting the life of Maria de'Medici painted for the Luxembourg between 1622 and 1625 and destined to have a lasting impact upon French art from Watteau to Cézanne. Though the latter was to make more than a dozen copies of this great canvas throughout his career, the earliest of these is the only one devoted to the group at the left, which includes the figure of the king. Executed with the clearly delineated contours and meticulous shading one might expect from a young artist, it remains one of Cézanne's most highly finished drawings.

Even more numerous among works of this period are studies after the nineteenth-century master whose style owed most to Rubens – namely, Delacroix. Though Cézanne's early letters make no mention of either of these artists, he later confessed a deep admiration of their achievement. Moreover, as early as *c.* 1873 he began work on a picture which pays homage to both and upon which he was still working in 1893 and hoped to complete as late as 1904. This is his *Apotheosis of Delacroix*, which shows the great Romantic painter being carried heavenwards, like Rubens's Henry IV. Below appear Monet, Pissarro, Chocquet, and Cézanne himself, acknowledging the debt the Impressionists owed to Delacroix's pioneering achievements, especially in the realm of colour. Though Cézanne's several studies for

138 *Woman in Fur*
(after El Greco), 1879–82

this composition were never developed on a grander scale, their theme and conception testify to his ambition to create a monumental museum picture which might vie with those of the acknowledged masters of the past.

The decade of the 1870s shows Cézanne copying an ever-increasing number of Old Masters, with isolated studies after Perugino and Fouquet, Gerard Dou, and Domenichino occurring alongside the more familiar copies after Rubens and Delacroix. Already in these years, however, one may observe the artist concentrating upon certain favourite works and masters, who were to furnish him with inspiration for the rest of his career. Who were they? And what was the nature of the appeal they exerted over Cézanne's creative imagination?

Cézanne's documented relationship with artistic tradition embraces a bewildering range of sources, from the greatest Old Masters to the academic painters of his own day. Thus, among the reproductions found in his studio at his death were works by

Michelangelo, Rubens, Poussin, and Delacroix together with those after such long-forgotten figures as Chaudet and Le Ray. As Theodore Reff has observed: '. . . a motley accumulation; uneven in quality; both provincial and sophisticated in taste; remarkably varied in its range of styles and subjects; in short a faithful image of Cézanne.'

When one turns to the artist's copies and letters, however, several distinct preferences emerge. The latter are unequivocal in their praise of the Venetian artists of the sixteenth century – above all Veronese and Tintoretto – and the Flemish and Spanish masters of the Baroque. Thus, in 1902, Cézanne exhorts the young painter Charles Camoin to 'make some studies after the great decorative masters Veronese and Rubens'; two years later he confesses to Bernard that the greatest painters of all are 'the Venetians and Spaniards'; and, in the same year, he admits to finding Tintoretto 'the strongest of the Venetians'. To this list only the name of Delacroix need be added as the nineteenth-century master most often mentioned and praised in Cézanne's letters.

Though the artist made studies after most of these masters, only in the case of Rubens is there a clear correlation between his written comments on art and his surviving copies. This may be explained by a number of factors, the most obvious of which is the contents of the Louvre. Though Cézanne admired both Tintoretto and the Spaniards, he made no known copies after the former and few after Spanish masters, probably because both are poorly represented in the French national collection. Indeed, Gasquet records that, at the end of his life, Cézanne lamented having seen little of Tintoretto or of the Spanish master to whom he felt particularly drawn, El Greco – perhaps the one Old Master to anticipate most fully the abstract concerns of Cézanne's own art. Yet the latter's sole copy after Greco was done from an illustration in a magazine, as though to supplement the holdings of the Louvre.

Another anomaly among Cézanne's copies is the absence of works after masters he evidently admired who are well represented in the Louvre. The most notable of these are Poussin and Chardin, who together account for only four of his surviving copies. Both of these discrepancies may, however, be explained by the purposes to which Cézanne put these copying sessions. For, if he admired Poussin as a landscape painter and Chardin for still life, he devoted his attentions in the Louvre almost exclusively to representations of the human figure. Moreover, while Poussin and Chardin were acknowledged classical masters, Cézanne was most strongly drawn to the painters and sculptors of the Baroque. Recognizing in himself an instinctual

139 *Bellona* (after Rubens), 1879–82   140 *Medea* (after Delacroix), 1880–85

classicism, he turned instead to those artists of the opposite inclina-
tion, whose dynamism and vitality might enrich his fundamentally
classic art.

Cézanne's preference for studying the human figure introduces us
to the most important disparity between his written statements on art
and his surviving copies: namely, that more than half of these are after
sculpture, especially that of antiquity, the Renaissance, and the French
seventeenth and eighteenth centuries. Included among these are large
groups of drawings after Michelangelo, Puget, and Pigalle, in
addition to the Greco-Roman masters to be seen in the Louvre.

John Rewald has succinctly summarized the reasons why Cézanne
was especially drawn to depictions of the human figure in his repeated
visits to the Louvre. In these, he notes, 'paintings and sculptures
replaced living models, with the added advantage that they didn't
move. Furthermore, Cézanne never felt before them that paralyzing

163

awkwardness which always seemed to have oppressed him when he worked from a nude model.' Another feature of Cézanne's copies of this theme is that they are usually confined to the study of a single figure, except in cases where the artist was confronted with a sculptural group.

Characteristic studies after the figure of Bellona in Rubens's *Apotheosis of Henry IV* and Delacroix's *Medea* may serve to introduce us to certain of the qualities Cézanne most admired in the great figure painters of the past. In both cases the artist has chosen an image of great emotional intensity – even tragic fury – which may well have touched a deep chord in Cézanne's inner nature. This is apparent in the unstable pose, the quick turn of the head, and the vehemence of the gestures and expressions. Yet so great is both artists' command over form and feeling that these emotional extremes find supremely lucid expression in their art. In this respect, they afford an exemplary instance of intense passion brought under perfect pictorial control – in short, the essence of Cézanne's own creative struggles.

Four other copies by the artist, done at different stages of his career and after very different masters, reveal an even more complex

164

141 *Mercury* (after Pigalle), 1873–76

142 *Beggar Boy* (after Murillo), 1882–85

143 *Ecorché*, 1893–96

144 (below) *Young Slave* (after Michelangelo), c. 1900

145 (below right) *Milo of Crotona* (after Puget), 1897–1900

141
142, 143
145
kinship. These are a copy after Pigalle's *Mercury* of 1873–76, Murillo's *Beggar Boy* of 1882–85, the so-called *Ecorché* attributed to Michelangelo of 1893–96, and Puget's *Milo of Crotona* of 1897–1900. Though only the last of these is portrayed in motion, all four figures are made up of two opposing diagonals which converge at the waist and, compositionally speaking, form a mirror image of one another. As such they convey the impression of dramatic conflict reduced to order – or of both dynamism and equilibrium. Since one of Cézanne's most cherished ambitions was to reconcile these seemingly contending currents in his own art, it is not surprising that he was drawn to such prototypes among the Old Masters.

In choosing such subjects Cézanne grew increasingly attracted to the interrelatedness of the parts in each figure and the flowing continuity of the pose. This is apparent if one compares the evolution of his drawing style using these four examples. In the early study after Pigalle, the artist employs long flowing strokes to delineate the contours of the form, though these are already overlaid with other lines to intensify the vitality of the pose. In the study after Murillo of ten years later, this process has been carried further, with Cézanne abandoning the continuous contours of his earlier style in favour of short, broken strokes which stress the rhythmic unity of separate elements in the composition and open out the figure into the surrounding space. This is one of the most unorthodox features of Cézanne's draughtsmanship. Rather than isolating a figure through outline and planting it firmly in space, he regards subject and setting as part of a continuum, permitting them to interact by subtly varying the blacks, whites, and greys available to him when drawing until they function almost as colours in his paintings – creating a sense of relief, relating a form to its surroundings and establishing the surface harmony of the design as well.

In the very late drawings all of these tendencies are accentuated by a more fluid and elliptical approach to line. This now possesses a freedom and spontaneity which seem to release the figure into the surrounding space and surface of the sheet, as though no longer wishing to draw any distinction between them. Thus, in the study after Puget, myriad, swirling strokes encircle all parts of the figure in a continuous rhythmic flow which vividly evokes the dynamism and pathos of the original.

As these examples demonstrate, Cézanne was most attracted to those artists who saw things not in isolation but in context and for whom every pictorial element was viewed as part of a larger whole.

For him these were the great decorators – or 'constructors' – among the Old Masters, those for whom the abstract unity of a work of art came above all other considerations. 'Michelangelo', he observed, 'is a constructor, and Raphael is an artist who, great as he may be, is always tied to the model.' And in Cézanne's late drawings after Michelangelo's slaves in the Louvre may be seen the thrill he experienced when   *144* confronted with such surging physical energy seeking spiritual release.

Cézanne's admiration for the acknowledged masters of plastic construction also accounts for his preference for copying works of sculpture, where the relief of the figure is even more tangibly visible than in painting and where the continuity of the pose could be explored from a variety of points of view. This also explains his fondness for copying Baroque sculpture, often conceived 'in the round' and designed to be seen from different angles. Among these were French portrait busts of the eighteenth century, whose elaborately coiffured wigs afforded him exactly the impetus he sought to explore those complex, curling and interweaving rhythms that increasingly dominated his art in later years. But Cézanne's favourite sculptures during this period were by Puget and Pigalle. In the full, flowing forms of the latter's *Love and Friendship* (Ch. 1044–47) or the straining energies of Puget's *Milo of Crotona* he beheld emotional extremes of happiness or pain finding an almost ecstatic physical expression. More than thirty copies after Puget attest to Cézanne's admiration for this master; another fifteen are after the plaster cupid attributed to Puget in Cézanne's day. These constitute   *126* the largest number of copies after any artist in Cézanne's oeuvre. A fellow Provençal, who had been born in Marseilles, Puget excelled in containing the most extreme states of action or emotion within designs of an almost geometric clarity, exactly as Cézanne sought to do. 'There is something of the mistral in Puget', Cézanne reputedly told Bernard, 'he agitates the marble.'

Puget's counterpart among painters was unquestionably Rubens, after whom Cézanne made nearly thirty copies spanning all phases of his career. On the face of it, this may seem surprising; for the florid and extrovert art of the cosmopolitan Fleming, filled with allegory and learned allusions, would appear to have little in common with that of the unworldly and reticent Cézanne. But Rubens was also the supreme decorative genius among the Old Masters – an artist gifted with inexhaustible powers of invention and an unrivalled command of pictorial composition. In the radiant beauty of his colour and the

146 Page of studies, 1867–70

rhythmic vitality of his vast, life-assertive canvases Cézanne confronted an art of boundless energy and imagination in which every
element served to strengthen and support the flowing harmony of the
composition and the decorative unity of the picture appeared
uppermost in the artist's mind. In short, Rubens's dynamic creations
were the example *par excellence* of passion and emotion subjected to
the controlling powers of the intellect.

In his love of this master, Cézanne was well served by the contents
of the Louvre, where the Medici cycle in particular commanded his
lifelong admiration. The subject of one of his earliest and most
136 methodical copies, this great series of canvases was to inspire all his
later studies after the Flemish master, its surging energies and swirling
rhythms already fascinating Cézanne in the 1860s, when he filled a
146 number of his sketchbook pages with designs from his own feverish
imagination which emulate Rubens.

In the following decade, Cézanne discovered the three naiads

168

147 *Three Naiads* (after Rubens), 1879–82

148 *Struggle of Love, c.* 1880

149 *Bellona* (after Rubens), 1896–99

playfully towing Maria de'Medici's barque to shore in the sixth
canvas in the series. In their contrasting poses, interweaving gestures,
and opulent nudity, Cézanne beheld a solution to certain of the
problems which beset him in his bather paintings of this period.
These, too, he co-opted for his own uses, though never with Rubens's
felicity. Something of the Flemish master is apparent, however, in
Cézanne's *Struggle of Love* of *c.* 1880, where he imparts to a gathering
of bacchic revellers the effortless flow and inventiveness of pose of his
great predecessor. Few canvases by Cézanne more clearly recall the
animated and continuous rhythms of Rubens than this. Yet even here
the figures are distributed in a frieze-like manner, their forms never
overlapping, and the whole is firmly bounded by framing trees in the
style of Poussin. 'Rubens and Poussin fought it out between them',
noted Gasquet of Cézanne, 'the abundance of the one, the order of the

147

148

150 *Naiad* (after Rubens), 1895–98

other, both haunted him together.' Gasquet's remark is both perceptive and illuminating; for the essence of Cézanne's creative difficulties lay in his desire to contain both of these contending elements in his own canvases, because both were contained in his very being.

Around 1880 Cézanne made his first studies after the figure of Bellona in the *Apotheosis of Henry IV*. During the rest of his career, he made no less than ten copies after this resplendent nude, and it is easy to see why. Not only does she demonstrate Rubens's masterly command of the human form in vigorous motion but she forms the very crux of the composition. Gazing mournfully towards the left, in homage to the ascending king, she veers boldly towards the opposite side of the picture, where Maria de'Medici receives the orb of the Regency. As such, she holds the entire design in her sway; and, in her

139

spiralling pose and voluptuous form, establishes a seamless transition between the two halves of the composition. In this respect, she performs the function of the presiding object in one of Cézanne's own still lifes, discreetly determining the rhythms and relations of those elements which surround her and summoning them together, like particles in a magnetic field.

149   In Cézanne's very last drawings of this triumphant nude, the figure is reduced to an ecstatic sequence of swelling curves which vividly evoke the organic unity of her pose. In these the artist explores the constructive principle which underlies Rubens's pictorial imagination and accounts for the seemingly effortless integration of even his most complex creations.

150   Even more remarkably, another late drawing reduces one of the naiads in the *Arrival of Maria de' Medici* to a simple sequence of stereometric curves, which at once express the torsion and vigour of her pose and relate it to the surface of the sheet in a manner that anticipates the formal devices of the Cubists.

But the profoundest lessons to be learned from Rubens concerned not merely the articulation of a single figure but that of the entire ensemble. For the essence of the Flemish master's genius ultimately lay in the remarkable unity of his canvases, where every figure and action appears coordinated with the whole and the entire picture seems permeated by a continuous plastic rhythm. This was a goal Cézanne constantly set himself and one which is immediately

135   apparent in his unfinished works, where annotations of colour and form indicate the abstract, rhythmic organization of the composition in advance of the objects themselves. Building and linking, these pulsing strokes of colour were the raw material out of which Cézanne sought to construct his own unified vision of the world – a quest which led him repeatedly back to the Louvre to consult the great sculptors and pictorial architects of the past.

CHAPTER SEVEN

Entering the Promised Land (1896–1906)

'Cézanne is very depressed and often attacked by fits of melancholia', wrote Numa Coste to Zola in April 1896. 'His self-confidence, however, receives some satisfaction and at auctions his works have a certain success to which he is not accustomed . . .' Unaccustomed though he was to the growing interest in his works which followed Vollard's exhibition of 1895, Cézanne's inner life changed little as a result. He was still prey to the same self-doubts, bouts of temper, and dramatically fluctuating moods. Age and ill-health were also increasingly taking their toll upon his constitution and occupying his thoughts. Added to these, he now faced a new source of irritation. In the wake of his recent successes in Paris, a growing number of young artists and critics, their curiosity aroused by his solitary habits, sought out the 'hermit of Aix', wishing to discover his theories on art or even purchase his paintings. Flattered though Cézanne may have been by such approaches, his ever-irritable nature soon led him to regard them with suspicion and his relations with many of these individuals gradually cooled. In the early stages, however, the artist maintained an active correspondence with a number of his new-found disciples of which we are the greatest beneficiaries. For the letters written at the end of Cézanne's life are the most numerous and illuminating of his career, both in the insights they afford into his own personality and to his ideas about art.

One of the first of Cézanne's acolytes of these years was the Provençal poet Joachim Gasquet, son of a school friend of the artist, who was later to write a series of reminiscences on Cézanne highly coloured by his own effusiveness. Initially touched by Gasquet's enthusiasm for his work, Cézanne made him a gift of one of his finest views of the Mont Sainte-Victoire and engaged in lengthy discussions *101* on art with the young poet. Before long, however, he had grown wary of Gasquet's attentions; and, accusing the latter of appearing to be angry with him, Cézanne replied in a letter of April 1896 with what amounts to a cry of pain:

Could you see inside me, the man within, you would be so no longer. You don't see then to what a sad state I am reduced. Not

173

151 *Self-Portrait, c.* 1895

152 (right) *Boy with a Skull,* 1894–96

153 (far right) *Peasant with a Blue Blouse,* 1895–1900

master of myself, a man who does not exist – and it is you, who claim to be a philosopher, who would cause my final downfall? But I curse the Geffroys and the few characters, who, for the sake of writing an article for fifty francs, have drawn the attention of the public to me. All my life I have worked to be able to earn my living, but I thought that one could do good painting without attracting attention to one's private life. Certainly, an artist wishes to raise himself intellectually as much as possible, but the man must remain obscure. The pleasure must be found in the work . . . Anyway, I am as good as dead. You are young, and I can understand that you wish to succeed. But for me, what is there left for me to do in my situation; only to sing small; and were it not that I am deeply in love with the landscape of my country, I should not be here.

Other letters of these years confirm the artist's deeply disturbed states of mind in the face of old age and infirmity – not to mention his ever-present creative frustrations. But perhaps the most distressing *151* testimony of Cézanne's inner torment is a *Self-Portrait* of *c.* 1895, which shows the artist recoiling from the viewer's gaze. Weary and pitiful, he resembles a wounded animal at bay.

The tragic overtones of this picture recur in many of the artist's late portraits, which are often melancholy in mood and sombre in hue and appear to reflect Cézanne's own inner states. As a further indication of the artist's increased solitude and isolation, most of these portray anonymous sitters – servants, farm-hands, and local labourers – in short, ordinary humanity. These were the only people with whom the aged Cézanne appears to have felt at ease; and it is through them that he imparted his deepest insights into the human condition.

One of these shows a youth seated at a table, meditating upon a skull, in the melancholy pose of the *Boy with a Red Waistcoat*. In *152, 119* contrast to the bright, clear colours of the latter, however, Cézanne here employs muted, autumnal hues which intensify the theme and reflect his own growing preoccupation with death. Melancholy of a more personal nature informs another of the artist's portraits of these years, the *Peasant with a Blue Blouse*. In this Cézanne portrays a humble *153* peasant seated before a decorative screen painted by him and Zola at the Jas de Bouffan in 1858–60 and generally regarded as his earliest work. This motif, with its obvious allusions to the artist's youth and long-lost friend, acquires added poignancy when one notes that the portion of the screen visible in the painting depicts a dallying young woman whose amorous suitor is concealed by the figure of the seated peasant – a substitution of youth and love by old age and loneliness that cannot have been lost on the nostalgic Cézanne.

But the artist's most haunting portrayal of human frailty of this period is the *Old Woman with a Rosary*. According to Gasquet, the sitter for this picture was an aged nun, escaped from a convent, upon whom the artist had taken pity, sheltering her and employing her as a servant. Even if this romantic tale is untrue, the abject figure of this woman clearly aroused the artist's sympathies. A devout Catholic himself, Cézanne confessed to his niece in 1899 'once old age has caught up with us we find support and consolation in religion alone.' Testifying to this belief is the artist's treatment of this forlorn old woman. Bent with age and sunken in feature, she clutches her rosary as though maintaining her last defiant hold upon life. Adding to the sombreness of the mood are the blues and greys which pervade the picture and the stiffness and angularity of her pose. These lend an almost oppressive feel to the work which mirrors the artist's dark moods of these years. An image of intense suffering and spirituality, the *Old Woman with a Rosary* is Cézanne's profoundest homage to Rembrandt – an artist he apparently studied at this time – and among his most deeply moving works.

A mood of ineffable sorrow also emanates from the artist's portraits of more fashionable sitters of this period. One of these portrays a woman wearing a flowered hat and elegant blue dress, seated at a table covered with a floral-patterned drape. In her strained pose and plaintive expression Cézanne explores an emotional realm far beyond the finery of her costume, much as he had done in the *Boy with a Red Waistcoat*. As in a traditional *vanitas* portrait – though without the allegorical trappings – he contrasts the fleeting comforts of youth and beauty with the inevitable disillusionments of life. These contrasts are even more apparent when one compares the shimmering blues and greens of the sitter's costume with the dark background against which she is seen. As in the portrait of Vollard and many other works of these years, the human figure emerges from out of shadow, a device which adds to the mystery and universality of the portrayal while also intensifying its atmosphere of prevailing gloom.

The most obvious exceptions to this are Cézanne's late portraits of his gardener Vallier. Though some of these depict the aged and humble figure seated in the studio, others show him outdoors, in Cézanne's own garden. Posed frontally and with a simple dignity, he is here reduced in size to make way for a view of his natural

154 *Old Woman with a Rosary, c.* 1896

environment – one in which he appears wholly absorbed through the greens and ochres of his costume and those of the surrounding foliage. The iconic simplicity of this scheme notwithstanding, these are Cézanne's most personal statements of this period. For they alone show humanity in harmony with nature, the artist's true refuge during these years.

Despite his growing 'success', Cézanne altered his working pattern very little during his last decade. As before, he continued to divide his time largely between Paris and its environs and his native Aix; though, as his health declined, he spent longer periods in Provence, where the countryside continued to arouse in him 'so many deep impressions'. In the summer of 1896 he spent two months in Taillores at Lac Annecy, where he made numerous watercolours and one of his 157   most remarkable landscape paintings, showing the view across the

156 *Portrait of Vallier,*
1900–06

lake with the Château de Duingt on the opposite shore. Dominated by the ethereal blues of the water, hills, and sky, which lend it a visionary intensity, the composition is itself remarkably simple, with its clear division between water and land, its vertical reflections, and large, framing tree. The colour, however, is of infinite complexity, with no two strokes of blue or green appearing exactly the same in size, hue, or direction. The prismatic effect achieved by this endows the picture with a transfixing stillness and mystery and creates the impression that the scene is forming itself before our very eyes.

This impression is enhanced by the different degrees of definition accorded to elements in the picture. Thus, while the house and château on the distant shore are clearly delineated, the landscape around them appears in an inchoate state, as though still awaiting further resolution. These relative degrees of finish within a single

157 *Lac d'Annecy*, 1896

painting imbue Cézanne's canvases with a sense of 'becoming' very different from that of his fellow Impressionists. In a landscape by Monet or Pissarro, for instance, all aspects of the picture are subjected to a more uniform treatment, with foreground elements stressed and those in the distance treated more summarily to enhance the illusionistic qualities of the scene. In Cézanne, however, objects at different points in space assert themselves while those around them often appear in a more embryonic state. This results from what the artist repeatedly referred to as his difficulties in 'realization' – of finding exactly the right tone and hue to render an object distinctly and relate it to those around. To our eyes, however, these varying degrees of completeness in Cézanne's pictures endow them with an unparalleled vitality and lay bare the formative processes of painting as few other works of art do.

158 *The Road at Montgeroult*, 1898

The brilliantly faceted effect of the *Lac d'Annecy*, with its increased fragmentation of objects and delicate modulations of hue, arises from Cézanne's own concern in later years (as he confessed to his son in August 1906) to put 'in as much inter-relation as possible.' In another letter, written three weeks later, he admits that the essence of his difficulties is in finding pictorial equivalents for the infinite variety of nature:

> Finally I must tell you that as a painter I am becoming more clear-sighted before nature, but that with me the realization of my sensations is always painful. I cannot attain the intensity that is unfolded before my senses. I have not the magnificent richness of colouring that animates nature.

Seeking to embrace all of nature's intensity in his pictures, Cézanne inevitably experienced frustration and defeat. Face to face with one of his landscapes of these years, however, it is hard to think of another artist who possessed more of the 'magnificent richness' of nature.

158 The transitional nature of Cézanne's art at this time may be seen in another landscape of this period, *The Road at Montgeroult*, painted on a visit to the north of France in 1898. The solid, geometric shapes of the buildings in the upper portion of this picture recall such severely architectonic landscapes of the mid-1880s as the artist's views of Gardanne. Combined with them, however, are the largely unformed passages of vegetation below, which exhibit a breadth and freedom characteristic of the artist's final years. At once evoking the animated and unpredictable forms of the natural world, they also reveal Cézanne's increasingly passionate response to nature during these years and possess a surging energy and lyricism which convey the artist's own exhilaration before his subject. In this respect, both sides of Cézanne's character – the classic and romantic – come together in this arresting canvas.

Returning to Aix later in 1898, Cézanne faced the one major upheaval of these years. In 1897, his mother had died, leaving her estate to be divided equally among Cézanne and his two sisters. This inevitably meant that the Jas de Bouffan had to be sold, depriving the artist not only of a place to live and work laden with memories of the past but also of one of the perennial motifs of his art. The sale took place in 1899 and the artist then moved to a small apartment in the centre of Aix, 23 rue Boulegon, where he resided for the rest of his life. Lacking a studio or a house in the country, Cézanne was moved in these years to make ever more ambitious journeys into the

159 *Rocks and Cavern II*, 1895–1900

surrounding countryside where he might work undisturbed and explore hitherto unfamiliar sites.

Two of his favourite motifs lay to the east of the town, in the direction of the Mont Sainte-Victoire. One of these was the abandoned quarry at Bibémus, above the village of Le Tholonet, where he worked at the end of the 1890s, painting dramatic views of the orange-red rocks of the quarry, whose jagged contours and massive shapes, rent with deep clefts, loom imposingly against the clear, blue sky. In one of the most majestic of these, the silhouette of the Mont Sainte- *164* Victoire rises above the quarry like a miraculous vision, recalling those geological upheavals which originally shaped our planet. Other works – including a group of watercolours – focus solely upon the complex and metamorphic patterns of the rocks. In certain of these the artist deciphers the bizarre contours of a human face – proof (if it *159* were needed) of his romantic identification with nature.

Another favourite site of these years was the Château Noir and its surrounding parkland, located halfway between Aix and Le Tholonet. Situated on a wooded slope overlooking the town, this uninhabited estate was also known as the 'Château du Diable' because

160 *Mont Sainte-Victoire*, 1900–06

161 *Mont Sainte-Victoire*, 1900–06

162 View of the Mont Sainte-Victoire from the Hill at Les Lauves

163 *Mont Sainte-Victoire, c.* 1900

164 *Mont Sainte-Victoire from the Quarry at Bibémus*, 1898–1900

165 *Le Château Noir*, 1900–04

166 *Park at the Château Noir, c.* 1900

legend had it that it had been built by an alchemist in league with the
devil. Cézanne painted five views of this house during the last years of
his life (V. 667, 794–97), which show its crumbling facade concealed   *165*
by dense foliage like some sinister relic of the ancient past gradually
being reclaimed by nature. Equally numerous are views of the forest
surrounding the estate, an inaccessible site full of large boulders and
closely growing trees, where the artist could be certain of working
undisturbed. In this secluded and impenetrable spot, untouched by
man, nature appeared to re-enact the elemental struggle for survival.

In one of these pictures (V. 787) Cézanne confined himself to a
monochromatic palette of greys, browns, and deep greens to convey
the brooding mystery of the site, finding solace for his own
melancholy moods in the oppressive grandeur of nature. Others
employ a more varied palette of warm ochres and vibrant greens and   *166*

167 *Great Bathers*, 1895–1906

168 *Great Bathers*, 1898–1906

169 *Great Bathers, c.* 1906

vividly evoke the primeval power of the living world in all its harshness and splendour. Whatever their mood, however, these pictures reveal Cézanne's deep attachment to his native countryside and recall his words to Gasquet in a letter of July 1896:

> . . . I commend myself to you and your kind remembrance so that the links which bind me to this old native soil, so vibrant, so austere, reflecting the light so as to make one screw up one's eyes and filling with magic the receptacle of our sensations, do not snap and detach me, so to speak, from the earth whence I have imbibed so much even without knowing it.

Cézanne's affinity with the landscape around the Château Noir even led him to attempt to purchase this property from its owner – an offer which was rejected. The artist succeeded, however, in renting a portion of the building, where he could store his painting materials and work when he wished. Seeking a more permanent studio, Cézanne purchased a modest property on a hillside site at Les Lauves, north of Aix, in November 1901. There he had a small two-storey studio built for him by September the following year. In addition to affording him with a place of his own, where he might paint still lifes and figure compositions indoors, this studio – now open to the public as a museum – commanded the most spectacular views. To the south Cézanne could glimpse a panoramic view of the town of Aix dominated by the cathedral of Saint-Sauveur; while, climbing up the hill to the north of this building, he could behold the most dramatic of all views of the Mont Sainte-Victoire, rising above a limitless expanse of fields and trees in isolated splendour. This awe-inspiring sight was to exert an almost obsessional fascination upon him during his very last years.

Cézanne had other motives for wishing to acquire a studio at this time. Around 1895 he had begun work on a large canvas of female bathers upon which he laboured for the next ten years, both in Paris and Provence. With the sale of the Jas de Bouffan and his move to the centre of the town, there was no space at his disposal big enough to accommodate this picture. During the following years, Cézanne embarked upon two more major canvases on this theme, in addition to producing a variety of smaller compositions of bathers in all media. Taken together, these comprise the most ambitious undertaking of his entire career. Though the artist had been occupied with the bathers theme since the early 1870s, the three great canvases of this subject dating from the last decade of his career were clearly intended as his artistic testament. In size, theme, and design they afford the clearest indication that Cézanne wished his art to be judged alongside that of the greatest Old Masters, for whom the theme of the nude figure in a landscape had afforded one of the supreme creative challenges.

Though the chronology of the three major bather paintings is difficult to establish, evidence suggests that the Barnes canvas was begun c. 1895 and the London picture four or five years later and that both were worked on intermittently until the artist's death in 1906. The Philadelphia version, on the other hand, only appears to have been started in that year. Internal evidence also supports this; for while the first two are heavily worked and show extensive signs of revision, the last is more thinly painted and appears to have been executed rapidly.

190

170 *Bathers, c.* 1900

Placed in this sequence, the three pictures also reveal a clear progression in complexity and compositional control. For not only are the first two somewhat smaller than the Philadelphia canvas but the number of figures increases from eight to eleven to fourteen as the series progresses. In addition, the size of the figures is gradually reduced to make way for landscape – a development paralleled in the artist's late portraits of Vallier. Finally, the figure groups themselves evolve towards a more compact and coordinated arrangement, with the great canvas in Philadelphia exhibiting the most harmonious disposition of figures and the most satisfying relationship between them and their natural surroundings.

In the first version, Cézanne deploys the figures in a frieze-like *167* arrangement across the picture, with standing nudes to either side framing a central group of seated bathers. Certain of these figures, especially the group at the right, appear to flaunt their sexuality; while those in the centre react animatedly to the appearance of the brutally proportioned nude striding on at the left. These features make the Barnes picture the most erotically charged and narratively conceived of the three and relate it to Cézanne's female bather pictures of the preceding years, especially to two slightly earlier oil sketches (V. 539 & 540) which likewise depict a lively gathering of eight female

171 *Apples, Bottles, Chair Back*, 1902–06

172 *Still Life with Apples and Oranges, c.* 1898

figures. The presence of an elaborate still life in the foreground of the composition, including a basket of fruit and a reclining dog, also appears reminiscent of the art of Manet and recalls the origins of this theme in Cézanne's early years. Similarly, the thick and tortured application of paint and the densely wooded landscape setting give the picture an oppressive feel reminiscent of the cathartic figure paintings of the 1860s.

The London canvas is both lighter in tone and brighter in hue and, *168* with its more spacious landscape and self-absorbed figures, appears less emotionally burdened. Unlike the Barnes canvas, the majority of the figures are seen in profile or back view, concealing their sexuality, and the animated poses and still-life elements of the earlier picture have been greatly reduced. The result is a more contemplative treatment of the theme in which two pyramidal groups of bathers converge upon the centre of the composition surrounded by a background of clouds and trees which supports this arrangement. At the far right, a small, striding figure bears witness to Cézanne's desire to create a more complex construction of figures located in different planes, in the manner of Rubens or Poussin.

Several features of the London canvas are worth considering in relation to Cézanne's other works of these years and to those of the Old Masters. Though the landscape of this picture possesses the lustre and intensity of his late paintings from nature, its imaginary origins are evident in the broad areas of local colour – white, blue, or green – which fill the scene. These differ from the intricately intermingled hues characteristic of Cézanne's independent landscape paintings of this period and testify to its more conceptual nature.

When one moves to compare this picture with the art of Cézanne's predecessors, several startling differences emerge. Among these are the frequent repetitions of pose, the wilfully limited palette, and the virtual absence of those blandishments for the eye which the Old Masters employed to enrich and enliven such scenes – flowing draperies, opulent still lifes, episodic figure groups, and a rich and diversified landscape. Certain of these omissions may be attributed to Cézanne's own limited powers of invention and occasionally result in congested figure groups of identically posed bathers placed side by side, as in the centre right of the London canvas. But others appear to stem from a deliberate decision to concentrate upon essentials and to create a monumental composition of female bathers devoid of specifics, whether of time, place, or action. Instead, Cézanne transcends all the narrative possibilities of this theme in favour of a more epic manner of presentation – one which portrays humanity in harmony with the eternal world of nature.

This is particularly true of the final canvas in the series, where the figures are arranged in two compact groups to either side of a spacious landscape, which affords sufficient indications of a setting to make nature a genuine protagonist in the scene, but not enough to suggest a precise location. Completing this impression of harmonious coexistence between man and nature are the framing trees which meet at the centre, like the arches of a Gothic vault, linking the figure groups below and mirroring the outstretched arms of the central bathers. Reduced in size and bulk from those of the two previous canvases, these now possess a serenity and spirituality that represent the artist's ultimate conquest over this most emotionally charged of all his pictorial themes. This is likewise apparent in the pale, unearthly blues, whites, and greens that pervade the picture. Thinly applied over a white ground, these lend it an air of remoteness and tranquillity appropriate to the artist's final meditation on this theme. No other work of Cézanne's career expresses more fully or movingly his own belief in the existence of an indissoluble bond between man and nature.

If the scale and complexity of Cézanne's late bather pictures invite comparison with the art of the past, other features of these works anticipate that of the future. Among these are the simplified and schematic drawing of the figures, whose bulky contours and featureless faces possess a primitive power and directness which look forward to the even more radical distortions of the human figure found in the early art of Picasso or Matisse. Like Cézanne, these artists make few concessions to conventional notions of beauty and, rather than imitating nature, prefer to recreate it in the imagination, concentrating upon essentials, both expressive and pictorial. Cézanne himself appears to have been aware that he was forging a new formal language in his last works and often refers to it in his letters. Thus, in 1896, he confessed to a young artist: 'I have perhaps come too early. I was the painter of your generation more than my own.' Sensing that he was witnessing a radical revolution in the arts, he embraced the prophets of the new who recognized in him one of their spiritual leaders. As he noted to Henri Gasquet in 1898: 'You have no idea how enlivening it is to find oneself surrounded by a young generation which consents not to bury one immediately.' But his most eloquent admission of the part he had played in creating the art of the future is a single sentence recorded by Bernard. Questioned by the latter

173 *Still Life with Bottle and Onions, c.* 1895

174 *Still Life with Apples and Peaches,* 1900–04

regarding his role in the new movement, Cézanne replied simply: 'I am the primitive of the way that I have found.'

Cézanne's importance for the younger generation became increasingly apparent as critical awareness of his revolutionary achievement grew during these years. By 1899 Vollard had staged a number of exhibitions of the artist's works, which he noted proudly were 'beginning to catch on with the public'. At the sale of the Chocquet and Doria collections in the same year, Cézanne's pictures fetched respectable prices, with Monet purchasing one of his landscapes at the Doria auction for the record sum of 6,750 francs. Also in this year, Cézanne exhibited three canvases at the Salon des Indépendants. In 1900, another three works by the artist were accorded place of honour at the Paris Centenary Exhibition. Thereafter, he regularly participated in exhibitions both in Paris and abroad, exhibiting again in Brussels in 1901 and 1904 and in Vienna and Berlin in 1903. Inevitably, however, his work aroused the greatest attention in the French capital, when seen again at the Salon des Indépendants in 1901 and 1902 or the newly formed Salon d'Automne in 1904–06.

Not all of this criticism was favourable, with one critic noting of his submissions to the first Salon d'Automne: 'Cézanne, barbarian. One must first have admired a great many famous daubs before liking this carpenter of colour.' Three years earlier, however, another critic had observed more perceptively: 'Cézanne is not known to the masses . . . but for a number of years painters have been following him attentively. Many of them owe to him the revelation of what one might call the intrinsic beauty of painting. In Cézanne the interest of the subject is not in its story . . . but rather in the production of visual delight.' Whatever the response to his works, Cézanne pursued his chosen path, noting in a letter of January 1905: 'I work all the time and that without paying any attention to criticism and the critics, as a real artist should. My work must prove that I am right.'

Though Cézanne's creative efforts during these years were largely devoted to landscape and bather pictures, he also executed a number of still lifes. Inevitably less ambitious than his work in other forms, these permit one to chart his stylistic development during this period with especial clarity.

173   Around 1895 the artist painted his *Still Life with Bottle and Onions*, which employs the plain background and stable disposition of objects of his works of the preceding decade. In place of the apples and oranges included in those pictures, however, Cézanne here substitutes

125   onions, already familiar from the *Still Life with a Plaster Cupid*. The

curling green stems of these permit him to explore a sequence of curvilinear rhythms throughout the composition which are also apparent in the elaborately carved apron of the table and the convoluted folds of the napkin. In this respect, the picture heralds a preference for more decoratively conceived still-life compositions which Cézanne was to pursue in his final years.

These tendencies appear even more marked in the *Still Life with Apples and Oranges* of *c*. 1898. In this Cézanne sets an elaborate display *172* of fruit and vessels on a steeply tilting table covered with an Oriental carpet and white tablecloth. In the cascading folds of the drapery the artist uncovers a wealth of curves which animate the entire composition. Aiding him in this are the vibrant reds and oranges of the fruits, whose shapes and hues are echoed in the floral design of the pitcher and richly patterned rug. The result is a sense of exultation in the infinite bounty of nature that finds obvious parallels in Cézanne's late views of the Mont Sainte-Victoire and has aptly led Theodore Reff to characterize such still lifes as 'symphonic'.

Scarcely less sumptuous in its choice of objects is one of the artist's last still lifes, where carpet, pitcher, tablecloth, and fruit appear piled *174* on to the ornately designed table of the still life of *c*. 1895. Now, however, the mood is very different. Seen against a dark background and painted in a range of muted and deeply resonant hues, the familiar objects of this picture acquire an almost tragic cast. Mysteriously glowing against their sombre surroundings, they no longer speak of sensuous delight but, rather, of profound resignation.

The contrasting moods of Cézanne's domestic still lifes of this period are also apparent in two of the more unusual motifs to attract his attention at this time. In nearly a dozen works of his last ten years the artist portrayed one or more human skulls, at times set starkly on a *175* bare tabletop and, at others, piled high upon an ornately patterned rug. One of these, now in the Staatsgalerie, Stuttgart, depicts a skull and candlestick, the traditional *memento mori* familiar from the artist's youth. Haunted by a fear of death at this time, and feeling himself 'at the end of my strength', it is hard not to attach a morbid symbolism to such works, especially when they are compared with the ghostly appearance of one of his final self-portraits. Yet Cézanne is also *176* reputed to have regarded the skull as 'a beautiful thing to paint'. And in those instances when he portrays it with a floral-patterned carpet, the ornate curves of the skull echo those of the flowers, joining life with death and growth with decay, in a manner that recalls his late views of the Château Noir.

Also among the artist's late still lifes is a group of flower-pieces notable for their colouristic richness and the wealth and density of their blooms. Unlike comparable works of the mid-1880s, where a vase of flowers appears as part of a larger assemblage of still-life objects, the late works portray this motif at close range. One of the most joyous of them is a copy of a watercolour by Delacroix that Vollard gave Cézanne in 1902. In this Cézanne transforms the detailed naturalism of the original into myriad touches of unblended colour which fill the picture field in riotous profusion. Paying one last homage to the great Romantic master, Cézanne here attains a vibrancy and animation of colour and brushwork comparable to those of certain of his later landscapes. For, among the artist's final still-life subjects, only the flower-pieces afforded him the wealth and intensity of sensations that he regularly experienced before a motif in nature.

The flickering, disconnected strokes and infinite modulations of hue of this flower-piece are also evident in Cézanne's late still-life

177

175 *Pyramid of Skulls, c.* 1900

176 *Self-Portrait*, 1897–1900

watercolours, where the lightness and transparency of the medium lend an insubstantial quality to all of the objects depicted. In one, of 1902–06, cursive pencil strokes indicate the approximate contours of *171* the forms of fruit, vessels, and an ornately carved chair. These are then overlaid with a sequence of coloured touches which define the forms in a chromatic scale that moves from the white of the paper, here used to indicate the lightest point of the objects, to a descending series of yellows, ochres, reds, and blues, which represent their receding surfaces. Modelling through colour alone – and avoiding either black or grey – Cézanne attains a breathtaking luminosity in these works, also observable in many of his oils of these years. He also demonstrates two of the most important theoretical statements he made to the young painter, Emile Bernard, at this same time. Thus, in July 1904, he observed: '. . . in an orange, an apple, a ball, a head, there is a culminating point; and this point is always – in spite of the tremendous effect; light and shade, colour sensations – the closest to our eye; the edges of the objects flee towards a centre on our horizon.' And, in December of the same year, Cézanne noted: 'an optical sensation is produced in our visual organs which allows us to classify

177 *Flowers* (after Delacroix), 1902–04

the planes represented by colour sensations as light, half tone or quarter tone. Light, therefore, does not exist for the painter. As long as we are forced to proceed from black to white, with the first of these abstractions providing something like a point of support for the eye as much as for the brain, we flounder, we do not succeed in becoming masters of ourselves . . .' Seeking always to create form and space in his pictures through modulations of colour, rather than of tone, Cézanne not only abandoned traditional methods of modelling but also redefined the role of drawing in his art. Though often beginning his works with cursory pencil strokes indicating the basic disposition of forms, he ultimately relied upon colour modulations to define their contours and points of intersection. 'Drawing and colour are not at all separate', he observed to Bernard, 'while one paints, one draws; the more the colour harmonizes, the more the drawing becomes precise. When the colour is richest, the form is at its fullest. Contrasts and relations of tone, that is the secret of drawing and modelling.'

In the end, however, as Cézanne admitted to the painter Charles

178 *Self-Portrait, c.* 1898

Camoin in 1903, 'everything, especially in art, is theory developed and applied in contact with nature' – and this is where he expended his final energies. Though reason might have dictated that he work increasingly in his studio on still-life and bather paintings, in the face of old age and infirmity, it is landscape that dominates the art of Cézanne's last years. Much of this is devoted to the countryside of his native Provence; for, apart from brief visits to Paris and Fontainebleau in 1904 and 1905, Cézanne remained in Aix during this period. His wife and son, on the other hand, continued to reside in the French capital – a separation that led the aged artist to engage in an intimate correspondence with his son during the last months of his life. In these letters he recounts his journeys into the countryside during a summer of unbearable heat. Usually, in the late afternoon, a carriage would take him to a shaded spot on the banks of the Arc or to the forest of the Château Noir. Occasionally, tramps or children would approach him begging, and Cézanne would throw them a few sous. Otherwise, he worked in solitude, immersing himself in the inexhaustible riches of a landscape he had known for more than sixty years. 'As for me, I must remain alone', he confessed to his son, in one of the last of these letters, 'the meanness of people is such that I should never be able to get away from it, it is theft, complacency, infatuation, violation, laying hand on one's work, and yet, nature is very beautiful.'

The loneliness of Cézanne's final years is captured in his last *Self-Portrait*. Among all his treatments of this theme, it is one of the plainest and most untroubled and speaks eloquently of a man who, in later years, found salvation only through art. 'Art is a religion', he confessed to the poet Léo Larguier, 'its goal is the elevation of truth'; while in two letters of 1902 to the young writer Louis Aurenche, Cézanne described it as 'the most intimate manifestation of ourselves' and as a way of reaching the stars. Gazing calmly out into space, as though disemburdened of the earth, Cézanne here wears the serene and timeless expression of an Oriental seer.

The profound spirituality of this portrait may also be seen in many of the artist's last landscapes. Some of these, admittedly, return to the dramatic motifs Cézanne had favoured in the late 1890s. This is especially true of his final views of the Château Noir and of works like *The Big Trees* of *c.* 1904, where the intertwining branches of two great trees fill the upper portions of the picture as though locked in combat. In their wild, untrammelled energies Cézanne powerfully evokes the regenerative capacities of nature and seemingly draws his own strength from its remorseless vitality.

Also among Cézanne's favourite late landscape subjects were views of his garden, of the town of Aix seen from Les Lauves, and (above all) of the Mont Sainte-Victoire. Over two dozen works in oil and watercolour were devoted to the last of these motifs during the artist's final years. These fall into two distinct groups. In the earlier of them, of *c.* 1900, the mountain is seen at close range from the vicinity of the Tholonet Road or the Château Noir. Viewed from here, its massive face dominates the scene, towering over the countryside in a manner that Venturi described as 'almost menacing'. Enhancing the turbulent intensity of these works are their broad, summary brushwork and simplified construction, in which the convoluted contours of the mountain appear reiterated in the hills and trees below. In one of these, the forms of overhanging branches rain down upon the mountain peak in a torrent of dark, stormy strokes which evoke a mood of almost unbearable anguish. 'Passion prevails over contemplation', observed Venturi of another of these views, 'the serene vision of the broad valley gives way to the cry of the pent-up forces of earth.'

179 *The Big Trees, c.* 1904

The other – and more extensive – group of works portrays the mountain as seen from the hill above Cézanne's studio, where it no longer resembles the colossal elevation of the previous pictures. Nor does it assume the form of a blunted cone familiar from the artist's landscapes of the 1880s, painted from sites to the south-west of the town. Instead, when viewed from the north, the mountain rises to a solitary peak which, like that of a church steeple, appears to link heaven and earth. Before this magnificent panorama, Cézanne stalked his final sensations of nature.

'I progress very slowly', confessed the artist to Bernard in May 1904, 'for nature reveals herself to me in very complex ways; and the progress needed is endless.' Evidence of the 'complex ways' in which nature revealed herself to Cézanne during these years may be seen in his late views of Mont Sainte-Victoire, where the canvas often appears covered in a faceted sequence of multicoloured strokes of paint of a seemingly unfathomable complexity, which at once evokes the pulsing life of nature and its limitless mystery. Often patches of bare canvas show through, as though still awaiting an undiscoverable interlinking hue – an effect which adds a sparkle and luminosity to these works comparable to those of the artist's late watercolours. Though the abstract and primordial quality of these pictures was to exert a profound impression upon Cézanne's younger contemporaries, the artist himself clearly regarded them as creative failures – as incomplete attempts to capture all of the 'magnificent richness' of nature. 'Now, being old, nearly seventy years,' wrote Cézanne to Bernard in October 1905, 'the sensations of colour, which give the light, are for me the reason for the abstractions which do not allow me to cover my canvas entirely nor to pursue the delimitation of the objects where their points of contact are fine and delicate; from which it results that my image or picture is incomplete.' Uncompromising to the end, the aged Cézanne still strove after a means of expression that drained – and contained – his entire being.

Aesthetic considerations alone, however, cannot explain his obsessive attraction to this mountain in his final years. As his letters of the period indicate, this was also a spiritual quest that embodied his deepest emotional strivings. 'I am working doggedly, for I see the promised land before me,' he confessed to Vollard in January 1903. 'Shall I be like the great Hebrew leader or shall I be able to enter? . . . I have made some progress. Why so late and with such difficulty? Is art really a priesthood that demands the pure in heart who must belong to it entirely?' Three years later, in a much more despondent mood, he observed to Bernard: 'I am in such a state of mental disturbance, I fear at moments that my frail reason may give way . . . Will I ever attain the end for which I have striven so much and so long?' His fortitude and determination unbroken, Cézanne admitted later in the same letter: '. . . I am old, ill, and I have sworn to myself to die painting.'

The periodic bursts of exultation and despair evident in these remarks are likewise apparent in his last views of the Mont Sainte-Victoire. In some of these, the canvas is densely coated with overlaid touches of colour through which the forms of the landscape appear barely discernible, a painful reminder of the aged artist's creative torments – and tenacity. Others – especially in watercolour – possess a *160* delicacy and lyricism which appear infinitely consoling. Employing myriad flame-like strokes of colour Cézanne creates in these a kind of mystic notation – or visual music – to evoke the celestial harmonies of nature. In several oils and watercolours, the artist even inverts the contour of the mountain in a sequence of coloured touches which converge upon the bottom centre of the composition. These afford moving evidence of the indissoluble order which he believed permeated all facets of creation.

Most visionary of all, however, are those late views of the *161* mountain floating weightlessly over the plain, like some spiritual intercessor between man and the divine. In certain of these the hues of the land are discharged into the sky, with Cézanne wringing from them all earthly impurity and permitting them simply to ascend, ecstatic affirmations of both human aspiration and universal harmony. Works such as these communicate a mystical belief in the transcendent beauty of creation which justifies Rilke's assertion that Cézanne set himself before a landscape 'drawing religion from it'.

On 13 October 1906, Cézanne wrote to his son: 'The weather is stormy and changeable. My nervous system is very weak, only oil painting can keep me up. I must carry on. I simply must produce after nature.' Two days later, working outside near his studio at Les Lauves, the artist was caught in a violent thunderstorm and collapsed in the rain. Several hours later he was carried back to the rue Boulegon in a laundry cart and put to bed. Though he rallied enough the next day to work on a portrait of Vallier, he died a week later, on 23 October 1906, his wish granted 'to die painting'.

Epilogue

Space and surface, form and colour, classical harmony and romantic intensity, the immutable and the everchanging faces of nature – Cézanne complicated painting by trying to solve all of its problems at once. In so doing, however, he opened up untold possibilities for later generations of painters and soon came to be regarded as the father of modern art. How ironic that he reputedly confessed to Gasquet at the end of his life: 'I am dying without any pupils . . . There is no one to carry on my work.' In truth, so protean were the implications of Cézanne's art that few of the most advanced painters of the next generation could afford to ignore it. His 'pupils' thus became virtually everyone of consequence connected with the birth of early modern art. For Picasso he was 'like our father . . . who protected us'; for Matisse, 'a god of painting'. Klee regarded him as 'the teacher *par excellence*'; and even Kandinsky – who derived little stylistic inspiration from Cézanne's art – acclaimed him as an artist who had laid the foundations of abstract art by relegating the objects he painted to the status of pictorial things. 'A whole generation of otherwise dissimilar artists have drawn inspiration from his work', claimed the English critic Clive Bell in 1914. 'That is why it implies no disparagement of any living artist when I say that the prime characteristic of the new movement is its derivation from Cézanne.'

Cézanne's effect upon his contemporaries is already apparent in certain early works by Pissarro, his chosen mentor. But the first major figure of his generation to benefit significantly from it was Gauguin, one of the earliest collectors of Cézanne's pictures, among them the *Still Life with Compotier*, which Gauguin valued above all other works in his collection. This admiration led him, in 1890, to paint a portrait of an unknown woman seated in a pose familiar from Cézanne's portraits of his wife of the 1880s, against a background featuring the *Compotier* still life. In further homage to the elder master, Gauguin adopts Cézanne's parallel, 'constructive' brushwork in this picture, though he simplifies the colour modulations in the *Still Life* in keeping with the more two-dimensional concerns of his own style. He thus drew attention to the decorative features of Cézanne's art, which were

180 Maurice Denis, *Homage to Cézanne*, 1900

soon to make him one of the spiritual leaders of the Symbolist painters of the 1890s who had initially found inspiration in Gauguin.

Included among these were Emile Bernard and Maurice Denis, the latter of whom acknowledged Cézanne's importance for the group in his *Homage to Cézanne*. Exhibited in Paris in 1901, this shows a *180* gathering of Cézanne's admirers and disciples – including Redon, Bonnard, Vuillard, and Serusier, in addition to Denis – around the *Still Life with Compotier*. The result is a homage to Cézanne comparable to the latter's *Apotheosis of Delacroix*. Deeply touched by *137* this tribute from the younger generation, Cézanne wrote to Denis expressing his gratitude in June 1901. 'Perhaps this will give you some idea of the position as a painter which you occupy in our time,' replied Denis, 'of the admiration which you evoke and of the enlightened enthusiasm of a group of young people to which I belong and who

181 Paul Gauguin, *Portrait of a Woman*, 1890

182 Georges Braque, *Houses and Trees*, 1908

can rightly call themselves your pupils, as they owe to you everything which they know about painting.'

When Denis wrote, Cézanne's canvases still remained relatively inaccessible to a wide public. With the major showings of his works which took place in Paris in 1904–06, however, his crucial importance for artists of the younger generation became increasingly apparent. This was confirmed by the two memorial exhibitions devoted to the artist in 1907, the year after his death, when 79 watercolours were exhibited at Bernheim-Jeune in June and 56 oils and watercolours at the Salon d'Automne in October. (It was the latter of these exhibitions that made such a profound impression upon Rilke.)

Even before these commemorative events, Cézanne had attracted the attention of three of the pioneers of early twentieth-century art, Matisse, Picasso, and Braque. Unlike their Symbolist predecessors, who were principally drawn to the decorative elements in Cézanne's style, these masters were instead attracted to its most architectonic features. For Matisse, who purchased Cézanne's *Bathers* in 1899, Cézanne became a model of order and clarity in painting, whose example spurred him to explore effects of solidity and relief in his own

87

art in the years around 1900. Ten years later Matisse turned instead to the formal and colouristic unity of Cézanne's canvases for inspiration for certain of his most decoratively conceived compositions, among them *The Blue Window* (1913; The Museum of Modern Art, New York) which invites obvious comparison with Cézanne's *Blue Vase*. Though other artists of his time drew more far-reaching conclusions from Cézanne's art, Matisse alone maintained a lifelong interest in it which was truly comprehensive and deserves to be seen as Cézanne's rightful heir. For not only did he choose to follow his great predecessor in working directly from nature but he remained aware of the equal importance which Cézanne had accorded to both form and colour in building up the armature of a picture.

But it was left for the creators of Cubism, Picasso and Braque, to investigate the most radical implications of Cézanne's style – its analytical approach to form and its rhythmic accentuation of the entire picture surface through a series of interpenetrating shapes and colours which generate space while also stressing the autonomy of the picture plane. This revolutionary new style may be seen in Braque's *Houses and Trees* painted – in homage to Cézanne – at l'Estaque in the *182* summer of 1908. Braque's landscape far surpasses anything to be seen in Cézanne in its geometric simplification of form, its boldly faceted construction, and its ruthless compression of space, which here appears as solid and material as the objects which fill it. The result is an image which accords primacy to the pictorial world over any notions of visual reality.

Cézanne himself had anticipated this development when he referred to his own painting as 'the logical development of everything we see' – implying by this a mental alteration of a visual sensation done in the interests of the compositional structure of a picture. In his art, however, this still took place before a motif in nature and was intended to reveal an invisible truth about it. But in the art of his Cubist followers it came increasingly to be done without any reference to the visible world, thus severing that link with perceived reality that had united artists from Giotto to Cézanne and paving the way for the conceptual art of our own age.

Select Bibliography

The literature on Cézanne is extensive and the reader will need to make full use of the bibliographies provided by the publications listed below to discover its range. The fullest and most up-to-date bibliography covering all aspects of the artist's achievement is in *Paul Cézanne*, Museo Español de Arte Contemporáneo, Madrid 1984, 266–280.

Primary Sources

The standard edition of Cézanne's correspondence is Paul Cézanne, *Letters*, ed. John Rewald, Oxford 1976 (4th ed.). A revised and augmented edition, also by John Rewald and including a number of previously unpublished letters, was published by Hacker Art Books, New York 1984. All quotations from the letters used here are from the 1976 edition. An indispensable anthology of early writings on the artist is *Conversations avec Cézanne*, ed. P.M. Doran, Paris 1978. For a selection of criticism and commentaries on Cézanne dating from 1874 to 1963, see *Cézanne in Perspective*, ed. Judith Wechsler, Englewood Cliffs, N.J. 1975. Individually published accounts of the artist by his contemporaries include A. Vollard, *Cézanne*, New York 1984 (orig. 1914); *Joachim Gasquet's Cézanne: A Memoir with Conversations*, London and New York 1991 (orig. 1921); G. Rivière, *Le maître Paul Cézanne*, Paris 1923; L. Larguier, *Le dimanche avec Paul Cézanne*, Paris 1925; G. Rivière, *Cézanne, le peintre solitaire*, Paris 1933.

Catalogues

The standard catalogues of Cézanne's works are: L. Venturi, *Cézanne, son art–son oeuvre*, Paris 1936, 2 vols (paintings); J. Rewald, *Paul Cézanne: The Watercolours*, London and New York 1983; A. Chappuis, *The Drawings of Paul Cézanne, A Catalogue Raisonné*, Greenwich, Conn. and London 1973, 2 vols. A convenient – though by no means wholly reliable – catalogue of the paintings is G. Picon and S. Orienti, *Tout l'oeuvre peint de Cézanne*, Paris 1975. John Rewald is currently preparing a revised edition of Venturi's catalogue, which is certain to become a standard reference work.

Biographies

The most authoritative and up-to-date life of the artist is J. Rewald, *Cézanne, A Biography*, London and New York 1986. See also G. Mack, *Paul Cézanne*, New York 1935; H. Perruchot, *Cézanne*, New York 1958.

Monographs and Specialized Studies

J. Meier-Graefe, *Cézanne und sein Kreis*, Munich 1918; R. Fry, *Cézanne: A Study of his Development*, London 1927 (new ed., University of Chicago Press, Chicago and London, 1989); F. Novotny, *Cézanne und das Ende der wissenschaftlichen Perspektive*, Vienna 1938; E. Loran, *Cézanne's Composition*, Berkeley and Los Angeles 1943; B. Dorival, *Cézanne*, New York 1948; L. Brion-Guerry, *Cézanne et l'expression de l'espace*, Paris 1950; M. Schapiro, *Paul Cézanne*, London and New York 1952; G. Berthold, *Cézanne und die alten Meister*, Stuttgart 1958; K. Badt, *The Art of Cézanne*, London, Berkeley and Los Angeles 1965; R.J. Niess, *Zola, Cézanne, and Manet, A Study of 'L'Oeuvre'*, Ann Arbor, Mich. 1968; W. Anderson, *Cézanne's Portrait Drawings*, Cambridge, Mass. and London 1970; L. Venturi, *Cézanne*, London and New York 1978; J. Arrouye, *La Provence de Cézanne*, Aix-en-Provence 1982; M.R. Bourges, *Itinéraires de Cézanne*, Aix-en-Provence 1982; A. Barskaya, *Paul Cézanne, Paintings from the Museums of the Soviet Union*, Leningrad 1983; R. Shiff, *Cézanne and the End of Impressionism*, Chicago and London 1984; M. Hoog, *Cézanne 'puissant et solitaire'*, Paris 1989; M.T. Lewis, *Cézanne's Early Imagery*, Berkeley, Los Angeles, and London 1989; J. Rewald, *Cézanne and America: Dealers, Collectors, Artists and Critics, 1891–1921*, London and Princeton, N.J. 1989.

Exhibition Catalogues

Cézanne, Musée de l'Orangerie, Paris 1936; *Cézanne, Paintings, Watercolors, & Drawings*, Art Institute of Chicago and Metropolitan Museum of Art 1952; Arts Council of Great Britain, *Cézanne*, by L. Gowing, Edinburgh and London 1954; *Cézanne Watercolors*, M. Knoedler and Co., New York 1963; *Cézanne*, The Phillips Collection, Washington, D.C. (subsequently shown in Chicago and Boston) 1971; *Watercolour and Pencil Drawings by Cézanne*, by L. Gowing, Laing Art Gallery, Newcastle upon Tyne, and Hayward Gallery, London 1973; *Cézanne dans les musées nationaux*, Orangerie des Tuileries, Paris 1974; W. Rubin (ed.), *Cézanne, The Late Work*, The Museum of Modern Art, New York 1977; *Cézanne*, Musée Granet, Aix-en-Provence 1982; J.J. Rishel, *Cézanne in Philadelphia Collections*, Philadelphia Museum of Art 1983; *Cézanne au Musée d'Aix*, Musée Granet, Aix-en-Provence 1984; *Paul Cézanne*, Museo Español de Arte Contemporáneo, Madrid 1984; *Cézanne*, Isetan Museum of Art, Tokyo (subsequently shown at Kobe and Nagoya) 1986; L. Gowing, *Paul Cézanne: The Basel Sketchbooks*, The Museum of Modern Art, New York 1988; L. Gowing and others, *Cézanne, The Early Years 1859–1872*, Royal Academy of Arts, London 1988; M.L. Krumrine, *Paul Cézanne, The Bathers*, Kunstmuseum, Basel 1989 (English ed. London, 1990); *Sainte-Victoire, Cézanne 1990*, Musée Granet, Aix-en-Provence 1990; R. Verdi, *Cézanne and Poussin: The Classical Vision of Landscape*, National Galleries of Scotland, Edinburgh 1990.

Essays and Articles

Although the periodical literature on Cézanne is far too extensive to list in full, some of the most thought-provoking discussions of the artist are to be found in the form of essays and short articles, often by non-specialists, a few of which are listed here: M. Denis, 'Cézanne', *The Burlington Magazine*, 1910, 207–219, 275–280; M. Merleau-Ponty, 'Cézanne's Doubt', *Sense and Non-Sense*, Evanston, Ill. 1964 (orig. 1948), 9–25; C. Greenberg, 'Cézanne', *Art and Culture*, New York 1961, 50–58; R.M. Rilke, *Letters on Cézanne*, New York 1985. In addition, four of John Rewald's most important articles on Cézanne are conveniently available in J. Rewald, *Studies in Impressionism*, London and New York 1985, 57–187.

List of Illustrations

All works are by Cézanne unless otherwise stated. Measurements are given in centimetres and inches, height before width.

47 *Dr Gachet and Cézanne etching*, *c.* 1873. Pencil, 20.4 × 13.2 ($8 \times 5\frac{1}{8}$).Cabinet des Dessins, Musée du Louvre, Paris, Gachet donation
48 *Portrait of Pissarro*, *c.* 1873. Pencil, 10 × 8 ($3\frac{7}{8} \times 3\frac{1}{8}$). Cabinet des Dessins, Musée du Louvre, Paris
49 Camille Pissarro, *Portrait of Paul Cézanne*, 1874. Etching, 26.9 × 20.9 ($10\frac{5}{8} \times 8\frac{1}{4}$). Photo Bibliothèque Nationale, Paris
50 *Family in a Garden*, *c.*1873. Pencil, 25 × 21 ($9\frac{7}{8} \times 8\frac{1}{4}$). Present location unknown
51 *Painter at Work*, *c.* 1873. Oil on canvas, 24.1 × 34.2 ($9\frac{1}{2} \times 13\frac{1}{2}$). Private collection
52 *The House of Dr Gachet*, *c.* 1873. Oil on canvas, 46 × 38 ($18\frac{1}{8} \times 15$). Musée d'Orsay, Paris. Photo Giraudon
53 *The House of the Hanged Man*, 1873–74. Oil on canvas, 55 × 66 ($21\frac{5}{8} \times 26$). Musée d'Orsay, Paris. Photo Réunion des musées nationaux
54 *A Modern Olympia*, *c.* 1873. Oil on canvas, 46 × 55.5 ($18\frac{1}{8} \times 21\frac{7}{8}$). Musée d'Orsay, Paris
55 *The Picnic*, *c.* 1874. Oil on canvas, 47 × 56.2 ($18\frac{1}{2} \times 22\frac{1}{8}$). Tompkins Collection. Museum of Fine Arts, Boston
56 *An Afternoon in Naples*, 1876–77. Oil on canvas, 37 × 45 ($14\frac{5}{8} \times 17\frac{3}{4}$). Australian National Gallery, Canberra
57 *View of Auvers*, 1873–74. Oil on canvas, 44.4 × 34.6 ($17\frac{1}{2} \times 13\frac{5}{8}$). Mr and Mrs Nathan L. Halpern
58 *The Road* or *The Wall*, *c.* 1875–76. Oil on canvas, 49.8 × 65 ($19\frac{5}{8} \times 25\frac{5}{8}$). Private collection
59 *The Harvest*, 1875–77. Oil on canvas, 45.7 × 55.2 ($18 \times 21\frac{3}{4}$). Private collection, Japan. Photo courtesy Christie's
60 Armand Guillaumin, *The Seine at Bercy*, 1873–75. Oil on canvas, 56.2 × 72.4 ($22\frac{1}{8} \times 28\frac{1}{2}$). Kunsthalle, Hamburg
61 *The Seine at Bercy* (after Guillaumin), *c.* 1877. Oil on canvas, 59 × 72 ($23\frac{1}{4} \times 28\frac{3}{8}$). Kunsthalle, Hamburg
62 *L'Estaque*, 1876. Oil on canvas, 42 × 59 ($16\frac{1}{2} \times 23\frac{1}{4}$). Private collection
63 Camille Pissarro, *The Road at Pontoise*, 1875. Oil on canvas, 52.5 × 81 ($20\frac{5}{8} \times 31\frac{7}{8}$). Private collection on loan to the Kunstmuseum, Basel. Photo Document Archives Durand-Ruel
64 *The Road at Pontoise*, 1875–77. Oil on canvas, 58.1 × 71.1 ($22\frac{7}{8} \times 28$). Pushkin Museum, Moscow
65 *Three Female Bathers*, 1874–75. Pencil, watercolour and gouache, 11.4 × 12.7 ($4\frac{1}{2} \times 5$). National Museum of Wales, Cardiff
66 *Bathers in Repose*, 1876–77. Oil on canvas, 79 × 97.1 ($31\frac{1}{8} \times 38\frac{1}{4}$). Barnes Foundation, Merion, Pa.
67 *Portrait of Victor Chocquet*, 1876–77. Oil on canvas, 45.7 × 36.8 ($18 \times 14\frac{1}{2}$). Private collection
68 *Dahlias*, *c.* 1873. Oil on canvas, 73 × 54 ($28\frac{3}{4} \times 21\frac{1}{4}$). Musée d'Orsay, Paris. Photo Réunion des musées nationaux
69 *Still Life with Apples*, 1873–77. Oil on canvas, 19 × 26.6 ($7\frac{1}{2} \times 10\frac{1}{2}$). Private collection
70 *The Dessert*, *c.* 1877. Oil on canvas, 60 × 73 ($23\frac{5}{8} \times 28\frac{3}{4}$). Philadelphia Museum of Art
71 *Still Life with Soup Tureen*, *c.* 1877. Oil on canvas, 65 × 81.5 ($25\frac{1}{2} \times 32$). Musée d'Orsay, Paris. Photo Réunion des musées nationaux
72 *Still Life*, *c.* 1877. Oil on canvas, 60.6 × 73.6 ($23\frac{7}{8} \times 29$). Metropolitan Museum of Art, New York. The H.O. Havemeyer Collection, Bequest of Mrs H.O. Havemeyer 1929
73 *Chocquet seated*, *c.* 1877. Oil on canvas, 46 × 38 ($18\frac{1}{8} \times 15$). Columbus Museum of Art. Museum Purchase, Howald Fund
74 *Madame Cézanne in a Red Armchair*, *c.* 1877. Oil on canvas, 72.4 × 55.9 ($28\frac{1}{2} \times 22$). Bequest of Robert Treat Paine II, Museum of Fine Arts, Boston
75 *The Bridge at Maincy*, 1879. Oil on canvas, 58.5 × 72.5 ($23 \times 28\frac{1}{2}$). Musée d'Orsay, Paris. Photo Réunion des musées nationaux
76 *Avenue at the Jas de Bouffan*, 1878–80. Pencil and watercolour, 30 × 47 ($11\frac{3}{4} \times 18\frac{1}{2}$). Staedelsches Kunstinstitut, Frankfurt-am-Main
77 *Le Château de Médan*, *c.* 1880. Oil on canvas, 59 × 72 ($23\frac{1}{4} \times 28\frac{3}{8}$). Burrell Collection, Glasgow Museums and Art Galleries
78 Drawing for *Le Château de Médan*, *c.* 1880. Pencil, 26.4 × 30 ($10\frac{3}{8} \times 11\frac{3}{4}$). Kunstmuseum, Basel
79 *Self-Portrait*, *c.* 1880. Oil on canvas, 33 × 26 ($13 \times 10\frac{1}{4}$). National Gallery, London
80 *Hills with Houses and Trees*, 1880–83. Pencil, 31.3 × 47.3 ($12\frac{3}{8} \times 18\frac{5}{8}$). Kunstmuseum, Basel
81 *Portrait of Madame Cézanne*, 1879–82. Oil on canvas, 92.3 × 73 ($36\frac{3}{8} \times 28\frac{3}{4}$). Foundation E.G. Bührle Collection, Zürich
82 *Madame Cézanne and Hydrangea*, *c.* 1885. Watercolour, 30.4 × 46 ($12 \times 18\frac{1}{8}$). Private collection, Zürich
83 *Portrait of the Artist's Son*, *c.* 1885. Oil on canvas, 64.4 × 53.9 ($25\frac{3}{8} \times 21\frac{1}{4}$). National Gallery of Art, Washington, D.C., Chester Dale Collection
84 *Portrait of the Artist's Son*, *c.* 1878. Pencil, 21.7 × 12.4 ($8\frac{1}{2} \times 4\frac{7}{8}$). Art Institute of Chicago
85 *Self-Portrait*, *c.* 1883. Pencil, 21.7 × 12.4 ($8\frac{1}{2} \times 4\frac{7}{8}$). Art Institute of Chicago
86 *Self-Portrait*, *c.* 1880. Oil on canvas, 65 × 51.1 ($25\frac{5}{8} \times 20\frac{1}{8}$). Kunstmuseum, Bern
87 *Three Female Bathers*, 1879–82. Oil on canvas, 53 × 55 ($20\frac{7}{8} \times 21\frac{5}{8}$). Musée du Petit Palais, Paris
88 *Five Male Bathers*, *c.* 1880. Oil on canvas, 59.7 × 73 ($23\frac{1}{2} \times 28\frac{3}{4}$). Private collection
89 *Great Male Bather*, *c.* 1885. Oil on canvas, 126 × 95 ($49\frac{5}{8} \times 37\frac{3}{8}$). Collection Museum of Modern Art, New York. Lillie P. Bliss collection
90 *Still Life on a Table*, 1883–87. Oil on canvas, 71 × 90 ($28 \times 35\frac{1}{2}$). Neue Pinakothek, Munich
91 *Still Life on a Table*, 1883–87. Oil on canvas, 65.1 × 80.8 ($25\frac{5}{8} \times 31\frac{7}{8}$). Courtesy of the Fogg Art Museum, Harvard University, Cambridge, Mass., Bequest of Collection of Maurice Wertheim Class of 1906
92 *Still Life with a Vase of Flowers*, *c.* 1885. Oil on canvas, 55 × 46 ($21\frac{5}{8} \times 18\frac{1}{8}$). Private collection
93 *The Blue Vase*, *c.* 1885. Oil on canvas, 61 × 50 ($24 \times 19\frac{5}{8}$). Musée d'Orsay, Paris. Photo Réunion des musées nationaux
94 *The Gulf of Marseilles seen from l'Estaque*, 1879–82. Oil on canvas, 59.5 × 73 ($23\frac{1}{2} \times 28\frac{3}{4}$). Musée d'Orsay, Paris. Photo Réunion des musées nationaux
95 *View of Gardanne*, 1885–86. Oil on canvas, 92 × 73 ($36\frac{1}{4} \times 28\frac{3}{4}$). Courtesy of the Brooklyn Museum
96 *View of Gardanne*, 1885–86. Oil on canvas, 63.5 × 99 (25×39). Barnes Foundation, Merion, Pa.
97 *L'Estaque*, 1882–85. Oil on canvas, 71.1 × 57.7 ($28 \times 22\frac{3}{4}$). Private collection
98 *The Arc Valley*, 1885–87. Pencil, 12.6 × 21.7 ($5 \times 8\frac{1}{2}$). Private collection
99 *Mont Sainte-Victoire*, 1885–87. Oil on canvas, 65.4 × 81.5 ($25\frac{3}{4} \times 32\frac{1}{8}$). Metropolitan Museum of Art, New York. The H.O. Havemeyer Collection, Bequest of Mrs H.O. Havermeyer, 1929
100 *Mont Sainte-Victoire*, *c.* 1882. Oil on canvas, 58 × 72 ($22\frac{7}{8} \times 28\frac{3}{8}$). Pushkin Museum, Moscow
101 *Mont Sainte-Victoire*, 1885–87. Oil on canvas, 67 × 92 ($26\frac{3}{8} \times 36\frac{1}{4}$). Courtauld Institute Galleries, London
102 Nicolas Poussin, *Landscape with the Widow of Phocion gathering his Ashes*, 1648. Oil on canvas, 116 × 176 ($45\frac{5}{8} \times 69\frac{1}{4}$).

The Board of Trustees of the National Museums and Galleries on Merseyside

103 *Self-Portrait*, *c.* 1888–90. Oil on canvas, 92 × 73 (36¼ × 28¾). Foundation E.G. Bührle Collection, Zürich

104 *The Gulf of Marseilles seen from l'Estaque*, *c.* 1888. Oil on canvas, 80 × 99.6 (31½ × 39¼). Art Institute of Chicago, Mr and Mrs Martin Ryerson Collection

105 Auguste Renoir, *Mont Sainte-Victoire*, 1889. Oil on canvas, 53 × 64.1 (20⅞ × 25¼). Yale University Art Gallery, New Haven. The Katharine Ordway Collection

106 *Mont Sainte-Victoire*, 1888–90. Oil on canvas, 71.1 × 90.1 (28 × 35½). Barnes Foundation, Merion, Pa.

107 *Provençal Landscape*, 1885–87. Oil on canvas, 65 × 81 (25½ × 31⅞). Present location unknown

108 *Mont Sainte-Victoire seen from the Wall of the Jas de Bouffan*, 1885–88. Pencil and watercolour, 45.5 × 30 (18 × 11⅞). National Gallery of Art, Washington, D.C.

109 *Portrait of Madame Cézanne*, 1887–90. Pencil, 48.5 × 32.3 (19 × 12⅝). Museum Boymans-van Beuningen, Rotterdam

110 *Madame Cézanne in a Conservatory*, 1887–90. Oil on canvas, 92 × 73 (36¼ × 28¾). Metropolitan Museum of Art, New York. Bequest of Stephen C. Clark

111 *Portrait of Madame Cézanne*, *c.* 1890. Oil on canvas, 81 × 65 (31⅞ × 25½). Art Institute of Chicago

112 *Full-length Portrait of the Artist's Son*, *c.* 1885. Pencil, 49 × 31 (19¼ × 12¼). A.L. Hillman Family Foundation, New York

113 *Mardi Gras*, 1888. Oil on canvas, 102 × 81 (40⅛ × 31⅞). Pushkin Museum, Moscow

114 Studies for *Mardi Gras*, *c.* 1888. Pencil, 24.5 × 30.7 (9⅝ × 12). Cabinet des Dessins, Musée du Louvre, Paris

115 *Five Female Bathers*, 1885–87. Oil on canvas, 65.5 × 65.5 (25¾ × 25¾). Kunstmuseum, Basel

116 *Male Bathers*, 1890–94. Oil on canvas, 60 × 82 (23⅝ × 32¼). Musée d'Orsay, Paris. Photo Réunion des musées nationaux

117 *A Card Player*, 1890–92. Pencil and watercolour, 51.5 × 36.9 (20¼ × 14½). Museum of Art, Rhode Island School of Design, Gift of Mrs Murray S. Danforth

118 *The Card Players*, 1890–92. Oil on canvas, 65 × 81 (25⅝ × 31⅞). Metropolitan Museum of Art, New York. Bequest of Stephen C. Clark, 1960

119 *Boy with a Red Waistcoat*, 1889–90. Oil on canvas, 79 × 64 (31⅛ × 25⅛). Foundation E.G. Bührle Collection, Zürich

120 *Kitchen Still Life*, 1888–90. Oil on canvas, 65 × 81 (25½ × 31⅞). Musée d'Orsay, Paris. Photo Réunion des musées nationaux

121 *The Card Players*, 1892–94. Oil on canvas, 47.5 × 57 (18¾ × 22½). Musée d'Orsay, Paris. Photo Réunion des musées nationaux

122 *Man with a Pipe*, 1892–94. Watercolour, 51 × 32 (20 × 12⅝). Interart Ltd., Zug, Switzerland

123 *Still Life with a Basket of Apples*, 1890–94. Oil on canvas, 60 × 80 (23⅝ × 31½). Art Institute of Chicago, Helen Birch Bartlett Memorial Collection

124 *The Great Pine*, 1892–96. Oil on canvas, 84 × 92 (33 × 36¼). Museu de Arte, São Paulo, Brazil

125 *Still Life with a Plaster Cupid*, 1892–95. Oil on paper, 71 × 57 (28 × 22½). Courtauld Institute Galleries, London

126 *Plaster Cupid*, *c.* 1890. Pencil, 49.7 × 31.9 (19½ × 12½). British Museum, London

127 *The Bellevue Pigeon Tower*, *c.* 1890. Oil on canvas, 64.1 × 80 (25¼ × 31½). The Cleveland Museum of Art, The James W. Corrigan Memorial

128 Photograph of the Bellevue Pigeon Tower

129 *House with Cracked Walls*, 1892–94. Oil on canvas, 65 × 54 (25½ × 21¼). Private collection

130 *Portrait of Gustave Geffroy*, 1895. Oil on canvas, 116 × 89 (45⅝ × 35). Private collection. Photo Réunion des musées nationaux

131 *Portrait of Ambroise Vollard*, 1899. Oil on canvas, 100.3 × 81.2 (39½ × 32). Musée du Petit Palais, Paris. Photo Giraudon

132 *The Dead Christ* (after Fra Bartolommeo), 1866–69. Pencil, 17.7 × 24 (7 × 9½). Kunstmuseum, Basel

133 *Reclining Male Nude*, *c.* 1865. Charcoal, 31 × 47.5 (12¼ × 18¾). Art Institute of Chicago, Gift of Tiffany and Margaret Blake

134 Peter Paul Rubens, *The Apotheosis of Henry IV*, 1622–25. Oil on canvas, 394 × 727 (155 × 286½). Musée du Louvre, Paris. Photo Réunion des musées nationaux

135 *Preparation for a Banquet*, *c.* 1890. Oil on canvas, 45.7 × 55.3 (18 × 21¾). Acquavella Contemporary Art, Inc., New York

136 Detail from *The Apotheosis of Henry IV* (after Rubens), 1864–65. Pencil, 40.5 × 30 (16 × 11¾). Private collection

137 *Apotheosis of Delacroix*, *c.* 1873. Oil on canvas, 27 × 35 (10⅝ × 13¾). Musée Granet, Aix-en-Provence

138 *Woman in Fur* (after El Greco), 1879–82. Oil on canvas, 53.3 × 48.8 (21 × 19¼). Private collection

139 *Bellona* (after Rubens), 1879–82. Pencil, 45 × 26 (17¾ × 10¼). Private collection

140 *Medea* (after Delacroix), 1880–85. Pencil and watercolour, 39.5 × 26.1 (15½ × 10¼). Kunsthaus, Zürich

141 *Mercury* (after Pigalle), 1873–76. Pencil, 21.8 × 12.4 (8⅝ × 4⅞). Present location unknown

142 *Beggar Boy* (after Murillo), 1882–85. Pencil, 19.4 × 11.8 (7⅝ × 4⅝). Private collection

143 *Ecorché*, 1893–96. Pencil, 31.1 × 23.5 (12¼ × 9¼). Private collection

144 *Young Slave* (after Michelangelo), *c.* 1900. Pencil, 21.6 × 12.7 (8½ × 5). Private collection

145 *Milo of Crotona* (after Puget), 1897–1900. Pencil, 21.2 × 13.1 (8⅜ × 5⅛). Kunstmuseum, Basel

146 Page of studies, 1867–70. Pencil, 17.2 × 23 (6¾ × 9). Present location unknown

147 *Three Naiads* (after Rubens), 1879–82. Pencil, 31 × 45 (12¼ × 17¾). Private collection, Zurich

148 *Struggle of Love*, *c.* 1880. Oil on canvas, 37.7 × 46.3 (14⅞ × 18¼). National Gallery of Art, Washington, D.C., Gift of the W. Averell Harriman Foundation in memory of Marie N. Harriman

149 *Bellona* (after Rubens), 1896–99. Pencil, 20.9 × 12.2 (8¼ × 4¾). Kunstmuseum, Basel

150 *Naiad* (after Rubens), 1895–98. Pencil, 20.8 × 12.2 (8¼ × 4¾). Kunstmuseum, Basel

151 *Self-Portrait*, *c.* 1895. Oil on canvas, 46 × 40 (18⅛ × 15¾). Private collection

152 *Boy with a Skull*, 1894–96. Oil on canvas, 127 × 94.6 (50 × 37¼). Barnes Foundation, Merion, Pa.

153 *Peasant with a Blue Blouse*, 1895–1900. Oil on canvas, 81.5 × 64.8 (32⅛ × 25½). Kimbell Art Museum, Fort Worth, Texas

154 *Old Woman with a Rosary*, *c.* 1896. Oil on canvas, 85 × 64.8 (33½ × 25⅝). National Gallery, London

155 *Woman in Blue*, 1900–04. Oil on canvas, 88.5 × 72 (34⅞ × 28⅜). Hermitage Museum, St Petersburg

156 *Portrait of Vallier*, 1900–06. Oil on canvas, 65.5 × 55 (25¾ × 21⅝). Tate Gallery, London

157 *Lac d'Annecy*, 1896. Oil on canvas, 64.2 × 79.1 (25¼ × 31⅛). Courtauld Institute Galleries, London

158 *The Road at Montgeroult*, 1898. Oil on canvas, 81 × 65 (31⅞ × 25½) From the collection of Mrs John Hay Whitney

159 *Rocks and Cavern II*, 1895–1900. Pencil and watercolour, 31.9 × 48.5 ($12\frac{1}{2}$ × $19\frac{1}{8}$). Private collection
160 *Mont Sainte-Victoire*, 1900–06. Watercolour, 36.2 × 54.9 ($14\frac{1}{4}$ × $21\frac{5}{8}$). Tate Gallery, London 1992
161 *Mont Sainte-Victoire*, 1900–06. Oil on canvas, 60 × 72 ($23\frac{5}{8}$ × $28\frac{3}{4}$). Kunstmuseum, Basel
162 View of the Mont Sainte-Victoire from the Hill at Les Lauves. Photograph.
163 *Mont Sainte-Victoire*, c. 1900. Oil on canvas, 65.6 × 81 ($25\frac{3}{4}$ × $31\frac{7}{8}$). Bridgestone Museum of Art, Tokyo
164 *Mont Sainte-Victoire from the Quarry at Bibémus*, 1898–1900. Oil on canvas, 64.8 × 81.3 ($25\frac{1}{2}$ × 32). Baltimore Museum of Art, Bequest of Miss Etta and Dr Claribel Cone
165 *Le Château Noir*, 1900–04. Oil on canvas, 73.7 × 96.6 (29 × 38). National Gallery of Art, Washington, D.C., Gift of Eugene and Agnes Meyer
166 *Park at the Château Noir*, c. 1900. Oil on canvas, 92 × 73 ($36\frac{1}{4}$ × $28\frac{3}{4}$). Musée de l'Orangerie, Collection Walter Guillaume, Paris
167 *Great Bathers*, 1895–1906. Oil on canvas, 133 × 207 ($52\frac{3}{8}$ × $81\frac{1}{2}$). Barnes Foundation, Merion, Pa.
168 *Great Bathers*, 1898–1906. Oil on canvas, 130 × 195 ($51\frac{1}{4}$ × $76\frac{3}{4}$). National Gallery, London
169 *Great Bathers*, c. 1906. Oil on canvas, 208 × 249 ($81\frac{7}{8}$ × 98). Philadelphia Museum of Art. W.P. Wilstach Collection
170 *Bathers*, c. 1900. Pencil and watercolour, 12 × 18 ($4\frac{3}{4}$ × $7\frac{1}{8}$). Private collection
171 *Apples, Bottles, Chair Back*, 1902–06. Pencil and watercolour, 44.5 × 59 ($17\frac{1}{2}$ × $23\frac{1}{4}$). Courtauld Institute Galleries, London
172 *Still Life with Apples and Oranges*, c. 1898. Oil on canvas, 74 × 93 ($29\frac{1}{8}$ × $36\frac{5}{8}$). Musée d'Orsay, Paris. Photo Réunion des musées nationaux
173 *Still Life with Bottle and Onions*, c. 1895. Oil on canvas, 66 × 82 (26 × $32\frac{1}{4}$). Musée d'Orsay, Paris. Photo Réunion des musées nationaux
174 *Still Life with Apples and Peaches*, 1900–04. Oil on canvas, 81.2 × 100.6 (32 × $39\frac{5}{8}$). National Gallery of Art, Washington, D.C., Gift of Eugene and Agnes Meyer 1959
175 *Pyramid of Skulls*, c. 1900. Oil on canvas, 37 × 45.5 ($14\frac{5}{8}$ × $17\frac{7}{8}$). Private collection
176 *Self-Portrait*, 1897–1900. Pencil, 31 × 24 ($12\frac{1}{4}$ × $9\frac{1}{2}$). Present location unknown
177 *Flowers (after Delacroix)*, 1902–04. Oil on canvas, 77 × 64 ($30\frac{3}{8}$ × $25\frac{1}{4}$). Pushkin Museum, Moscow
178 *Self-Portrait*, c. 1898. Oil on canvas, 63.5 × 50.8 (25 × 20). Charles H. Bayley Fund and partial gift of Elizabeth Paine Metcalf, Museum of Fine Arts, Boston
179 *The Big Trees*, c. 1904. Oil on canvas, 81 × 65 ($31\frac{7}{8}$ × $25\frac{1}{2}$). The National Gallery of Scotland, Edinburgh
180 Maurice Denis, *Homage to Cézanne*, 1900. Oil on canvas, 180 × 240 (71 × 95). Musée d'Orsay, Paris. Photo Réunion des musées nationaux
181 Paul Gauguin, *Portrait of a Woman*, 1890. Oil on canvas, 65 × 55 ($25\frac{5}{8}$ × $21\frac{5}{8}$). Art Institute of Chicago, Joseph Winterbotham Collection
182 Georges Braque, *Houses and Trees*, 1908. Oil on canvas, 73 × 59.5 ($28\frac{3}{4}$ × $23\frac{3}{8}$). Kunstmuseum, Bern, Hermann and Margit Rupf-Stiftung

Index